Ralph Bartholdt's writing and photography have appeared nationally and in regional publications throughout the Pacific Northwest. His work has been recognized by the Idaho Press Club, National Newspaper Association, the Associated Press and the Society of Professional Journalists. He lives in Idaho's Panhandle.

Also by
RALPH BARTHOLDT

Sometime, Idaho
Somewhere, Idaho

"This is the wealth of the world. And we are rich."

— Gene Hill

someplace, Idaho

Short essays from Idaho's panhandle

Grassy Mountain Press
St. Maries, Idaho

For permission requests write to Grassy Mountain Press, grassymountainpress@gmail.com

ISBN: 978-1-68524-445-3 (Paperback)

Library of Congress Control Number: 2021924967

Portions of this book are works of nonfiction. Some of these essays have appeared in *Northwest Sportsman Magazine, The St. Maries Gazette Record, Livingston Enterprise, The Billings Gazette, Missoulian, The Lewiston Tribune* and *Coeur d'Alene Press.*

Photos by Ralph Bartholdt unless otherwise noted.

Book design by Benjamin Riley.

Printed by kdp.amazon.com

First printing edition 2021.

Grassy Mountain Press

Gitta, Izzy, Emmi, Livvy, Reid

Contents

Autumn

Winter

Spring

Summer

Autumn

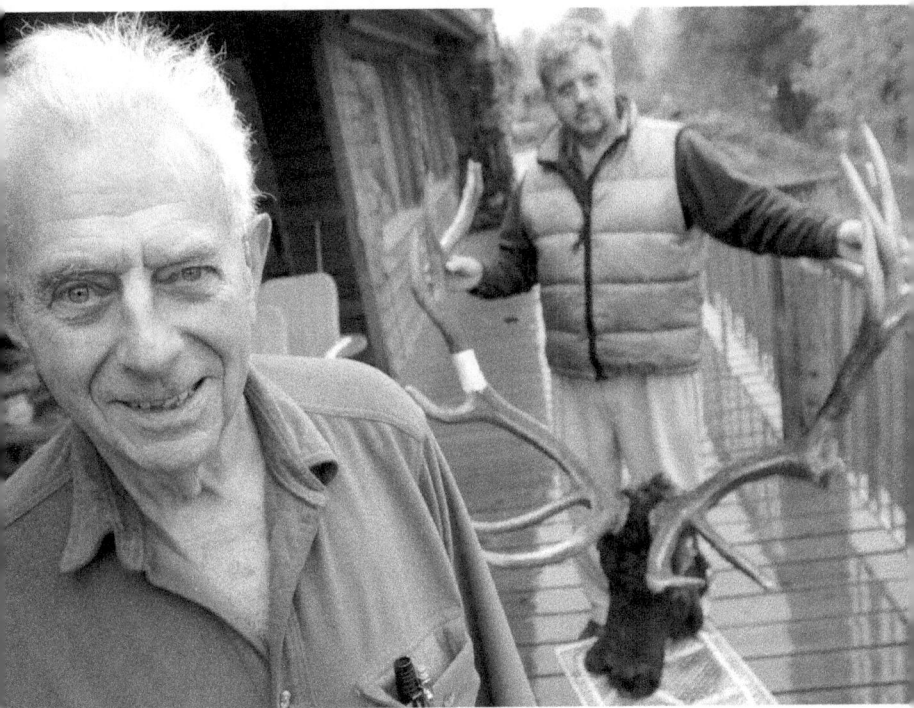

All Night Elk Hunter

I have always admired the guy who goes the extra mile during the fall hunting seasons. He's the one who takes a sabbatical from his job at the mill to ensure he has fifty eight days to hunt elk in places where no one has left a tire or boot track since the federal agents ventured there to scour the earth for pieces of a fallen satellite.

He chunks out ninety four days for the whitetailed deer season that starts in August about the time he cashes in the vacation and sick leave he's accrued, then tosses the steering wheel out the window and bids his coworkers adieu, until, well, that depends where this road takes him.

The razor arrows are in the quiver, the forest maps are colored with red and yellow felt markers and stuffed into zip-top plastic bags and most of what was in the garage freezer is stored now in portable, backseat coolers.

A blue sky lies ahead, but at this time of night the traffic lights on the highway leading out of town blink yellow.

He rises early if he sleeps at all, not bothering with the bathroom mirror, the cupboard with the perfumes and deodorants, shavers, the toothpaste tube. He rolls down the driveway without touching the gas pedal and through the neighborhood without turning on his headlamps, so as to adjust his pupils to the darkness right off.

His wife works the night shift at the corner gas station that doubles as a sporting goods store. You can sometimes find him there before the exhaust pipes of the logging trucks flutter, sipping coffee from a styrofoam cup, but usually not for long.

The kids are asleep, he tells her. He had grandma move into the spare room above the garage that was called an attic before he rearranged the boxes, added a space heater and screwed in a lightbulb.

It's not permanent. Gosh, no! It's just until the snow flies and the elk are hunkered down and the tags the rest of us carry in our billfolds expire.

Regular sitters are unreliable and costly, and he wants what's best for the kids.

He grabs an extra box of shells and face paint by reaching over the glass counter and when his wife interrupts glancing sideways at the surveillance cameras, he squawks.

She comes to assist wearily, mentally subtracting the cost of the items from her paycheck.

"Not those," he says, tapping the glass case. "Yeah, them there."

He rolls a handful of jerky into a paper towel from the quickie food aisle and finds a place for the bundle in the many pockets of the pants he keeps in a rubber tote most of the time, fermenting in elk urine.

He'll peck a kiss at his wife before the taillights of his family's all-wheel-drive blink through the four-way stop and down the road in directions undisclosed.

He's the one you see coming out of the woods before daybreak just as you're heading in.

The grass in his yard hasn't been cut since the early archery season and around Thanksgiving he's behind the house by the garden shed changing the plugs of the snowmobile, pulling the starter cord at all hours, firing the engine, tinkering, because during the muzzleloader season, "them elk are way back in the gnarly country, up high where the snow is piling."

He's the dad you greet with a nod in the school gymnasium in January during the little kid wrestling season, because at first you don't recognize him through his beard that looks like he spent a month dining at the feather pillow buffett.

"That you in there? Ha ha."

He is dejected now in February.

Just a little.

He doesn't let on.

"Filled the freezer," he says. "Put meat on the table."

Some of us rely on that to get us through the year, he moans quietly under his breath as if it's a rehearsal and he's learning the lines real well.

He wants the right inflection, so the wife will finally let him off the hook.

"Uh, huh," she says.

He'll have another job by spring, maybe on the forklift if they'll have him back at Spud Creek Lumber, he assures his in-laws and people like me who admire his tenacity.

The undercarriage on the SUV is just one of his wife's paychecks away from an inspection at Billy's Fix-It Quick. There's still the matter of the radiator where the cedar stob went through the grill in October. And he needs a tire to replace the pancake spare that rides too low. Oh, yes, the broken headlight too needs his attention, and the upholstery where the antlers of the young bull elk that didn't quite fit in the cargo bay left a mark.

He and another guy, equally untrimmed, snigger briefly at this before looking over their shoulders to make sure their secret stays secure.

Ever since November a small, black puddle has been showing up in the driveway, but no worries.

"A boulder jarred the oil pan way up on the state line, so it prolly needs a gasket," he mulls. "That's a cheap fix."

Too bad he traded his super mechanic tool set for that Idaho handmade rifle scope that's powered by starlight and reaches out crystal clear even when it's overcast, like bifocals on a barber's nose.

He's filled out job applications but hasn't distributed them just yet.

He repeats this glumly.

Just waiting for the planets to align.

It's shed hunting season, and at his age it's just

healthier to be outside than in some warehouse pushing merchandise around.

The rest of us worship his aimless prevarications that focus on the outdoors. They smell — we whiff it from across a couple of rows of bleachers in the gym — of cosmoline and cordite, pork rind, the essence of mink oil absorbed into cuticles, and pine needles.

Harvesting a sweet little forked-horned deer like we did last autumn because it crossed the fence from the barn heading to the apple trees, isn't really considered a hunt, now is it?

It helped us fill a tag and retain that piece of self esteem when someone asked, "How was huntin'?"

"Oh, you know, 'got a little buck."

There may be time, this coming season, for some of us to hike out before daylight and climb into a stand, so we can talk about the ones we saw, but didn't get.

"I heard him comin' and then, there he was, big as Texas, and I shot right over the top of him."

Elk season?

We hunted just two days last year, got into them, but duty, otherwise known as the missus or a steady job, reeled us back like lip-hooked bottom fish.

That's why we admire this guy who lived among the harems of big ivory-toothed deer, learned their dialect, scribbled their contact information into the recess of his guiltless brain, and basically went all wild-like for months without punching a time clock.

Whatever makes him tick, we would like a little bit of it. Just enough to box-step on the rim of disregard and peer into the caldera of gleefulness. We daydream of the freedom that considers the future mostly through the reticle of a spotting scope.

It takes a special courage to live like that.

Grousing, Gun Dogs, Goodbyes

HELLS GULCH — The German shorthairs were two. A mother and son often found loafing on a dog bed in the front room of the Tower News, a weekly tattler in a town somewhere north of the Laurentian Divide, but not so far that you would mush to get there.

They belonged to my Uncle Jim who, when he wasn't peering through ink-dusted eyeglasses at kerning or font, or the inevitable upside down of the linotype, took advantage of the place he was raised and a proclivity for guns and gun dogs that he inherited along with the dairy farm-like workmanship of the newspaper.

In his free time, he would hunt with zeal.

His dogs, big-bodied with ashen ticks, dark saddles and claws click-clicking on the wooden floor of the newspaper's front room, are now, in some circles, referred to as versatile hunting dogs.

Jim did not utter the phrase.

He called them by their given names and if there was a man from whom one could learn patience, Jim was it. At least when it came to his dogs.

They were used mostly on the grouse and pheasants that he would travel to find as time and the newspaper allowed, sometimes to Dakota and rarely to Montana.

I wanted an Irish setter as a kid, but when my friend's setter, named Red — a tribute to the Jim Kjelgaard series of books that a much different Disney popularized — slid off the doghouse roof on the snub side of a restraining rope, my pal's dad exclaimed, "Fool dog," and buried it in the backyard.

We believed him, my pal, Honer, and I. For this reason, Red was replaced not with another setter but with an American water spaniel, a breed also in the stable of versatile dogs.

We lived fine, Honer and me and his dog, hunting Sundays after church until dark. We ranged far afoot but were always home with supper: teal, maybe a Canada goose, squirrel, rabbit, ruffed grouse, burrs in our socks and in the dog's wash-n-wear fur.

Anyone with an affection for uplands and marshes has been around their share of dogs. Some of them, like Jim's dogs, are a pleasure. Honer's dog, Mick, was pretty fair, and a dog I raised for birds as a kid — a redbone retriever mix, always game with a strong nose and persistence — is memorable too.

A biology teacher I knew in high school taught a Brittany spaniel to work so briskly for grouse without a word, just a whistle, that days were spent hammering through aspen groves with nary a yell, just the whir of wings and a lot of gunshots.

"Easy now," and "good girl," was the extent of the conversation between dog and hunter. When luck, the dog's grace and a good shooting eye met, "fetch," and "drop" were most often spoken.

A Southeast Alaska logging truck driver with a biology degree had the first pair of Deutsch drahthaars I ever knew. They hunted geese in the salt flats near Admiralty Island. Before settling in a blind, the owner let the dogs loose in the marsh to find wounded ducks and geese.

"They'll make a run around the flats and retrieve the crippled birds that others don't find," the owner said.

Because of the drahts' audacious and selfless birding, the man sometimes filled his limit without cocking the hammers of a long-barreled fowling gun. He used his dogs to trail blacktail too, ptarmigan in the uplands and the blue grouse that sailed downhill from the tops of Sitka spruce trees to hoot and boom and be shot from low limbs.

The inimitable outdoor writer Charley Waterman dedicated a book to a dog. The Brittany he named Kelly hunted and retrieved twenty one species of upland game birds in North America. I remember the black-and-white pictures of Charley hunting chukars at sixty years old in the sharp rock and scrub inclines above the Snake River with his Brittany loping, ears back, and him slow at chase.

———————————

I buried my dog last week. I laid Matti down on a bed of tamarack needles on land I own where she was raised and chased wild birds, chickens and cats.

I didn't know much about Vizslas when I got her more than a decade ago, just that her coat was red like the dog I had as a kid. She was a pointer, and from Hungary. Game wardens used her breed harkening so far back into the volumes of European history you needed a loupe to read the big print.

I had grown up with dogs that didn't seek attention, just a pat when they brought back a bird, but this one was different. She was the infant with colic, the 24/7 cockatiel that wouldn't leave your shoulder, the howling and whining neurotic who mistook a dog bed by the door as purgatory and a dog bed in the garage as banishment. She sneaked to the couch and wanted the bedroom, played with the kid's chickens nicely, until you turned your back, then she quietly snapped their necks and buried them in the flowerbed.

She gave up the birds I shot only reluctantly because she craved the after-retrieve praises. She pointed when I was in sight, but would rather flush when I wasn't, driving birds over the mountain.

If I shot a deer but couldn't find it, she was brought to the place and unleashed. I ran behind her to some swamp or the bottom of a draw, or to the spot under the brushing arms of fir where the buck lay dead.

Our hunts in the later years ended in resentment. I was angry at what I mistakenly considered her lack of drive when there were no upland birds about, and she asked to crawl into my lap with her head to my heart to make up.

When she died at fourteen, I missed her immediately. Maybe for the places we saw together, the high trails and deep woods all over North Idaho, or the more than a decade of life that passed under our paws.

When we hunted, her coat blended so well with the osier and orange hues of autumn that she was collared with a bell, but her location was best charted by birds flying away.

I laid her slim body in a grove of tamaracks where we crossed a lot, and not far from the ruffed grouse drumming log of one particular bird we never got. I turned to look back, but she was gone. Her fur melding with the supple and perfect mirror of its surroundings.

I worked in western Alaska years ago where my boss, a man I surreptitiously called uncle, said there isn't a day you can't learn a thing or two from the lowliest truck driver. He said this over beers in a bar in Nome.

We learn from dogs that way, too, all of them. They tell us something once and it sticks. We may not like it but there it is. The wisdom of their eyes when they refuse a dimwitted command, their wanton determination, their need for lavishment, their virtue we don't deserve.

Pay attention, they say.

I am not a water dog, so don't try it.

If that bird breaks I shall leap into the air after it, so hold your fire.

My eagerness will make me topple down this cliff after a fallen partridge, but don't worry, I'll be alright.

Take me as I am, or don't.

They all have their own makeup and markings.

Their versatility lies in their acceptance of us, and they ask only that we be versatile too.

In The Same Current

PECK — The run began at a shelf that dropped into a thin, boiling line and smoothed out along a cut bank below the railroad tracks.

It unspooled itself for a hundred yards and then fanned wide beneath a steel bridge.

It was noisy with the current funneling from the main stem of the Clearwater River east of Lewiston, through braids and veins before rejoining.

The smooth, round rocks were slippery underfoot as I stood ankle-deep and whirled the fifteen-foot rod, a ten-weight that was loaned to me as a learning tool. I made the sweeping loops that a fishing guide once in a bar over river beer explained as painting the ceiling.

"Think of your rod tip as a brush and you're painting the ceiling," he said to a client who was painfully urbane and definitely foreign to the region, and who had likely paid the guide nicely to fish but was instead dragged to a bar to drink beer and talk about fishing.

The client sipped and patiently listened as the guide waved his arms in animation while rain painted lines on the windows.

Everyone in the place had suspected it then, and I was learning it now. You don't pretend to paint a ceiling or anything else with the tip of an ungainly spey rod. Casting requires a brief and exaggerated movement followed by a swift but snappy stroke that loads the rod before shooting a ton of long-belly floating line through the rod guides with gusto. The heavy line zings across a big chunk of dark water like a flock of low-flying birds and lands way out there with precision, not in a curlicue of mono.

The fly at the tail of this presentation alights gracefully, but also with abrupt conclusion, like the Flamenco.

Then you let it swing and watch as the fly skates on water.

When it nears shore you take a step or two downriver while stripping excess line. Then repeat the ritual like a prairie grouse dancing and cooing bizarrely in morning's first light.

Standing on this particular shelf across from the railroad tracks, turning my body to watch the spey line squiggle in the current and the topwater fly swing downriver leaving a wake, I spied the small figure of a man walking my way.

He picked his way patiently over the rocks.

I flummoxed another cast and let whatever I had out there, pig-tailed leader and fly, the whole amalgam of nylon and feathers and steel, swing in whatever fashion physics allowed and the man kept coming.

I did this for a while, floundering a cast, swinging, stepping, and watching downstream before I reeled in and met the man halfway.

There was no one else around. It was early. The morning sun had just peaked over a treeless ridge, grass-brown and shorn as a cantaloupe. The golden light was a sudden explosion, but silent. And the man, an elderly gentleman, fit, with a worn baseball cap who carried a rod at least as long as mine, kept coming.

He was from San Francisco. A retired engineer, he said. He was taut and had the look of someone accustomed to leaning against the current of rivers. He cast at the Golden Gate Club, he explained and had walked all the way up the edge of the island, this man of fly-casting erudition, to ask if I, a novice, would allow him to fish nearby.

"Are you fishing all the way through?" he asked.

"I'm not sure," I said.

I wasn't. I hadn't thought much about it. I was more attuned to my cast and knew that because it was a work day I would have to be in the office in an hour. I would fish as far downstream as time allowed, I told the man.

"OK," he said, before explaining that the run below us — it seemed a quarter mile away — was not connected to the run I had been fishing.

"I think they are two separate runs," the man with the faded ball cap said.

This was my introduction to the stream ethics of spey fishing on the Clearwater River and probably anywhere.

The man then took my rod and presented me with a fifteen-minute casting lesson. The river flushed around us, there was no one else in sight. Logging trucks flashed on the highway through the cottonwoods and the sun threw its golden rays over our heads and into the rising fog like a mist net.

The man showed me a snake roll explaining that wind, more so than in single-handed fly casting, is an enemy worth recognizing.

"I had a hook strike me in the head," he said.

He had not considered the wind when he swung his two-handed rod, decades ago, nor the heft of the big fly on the end of it.

"It knocked my hat off," he said. "I saw stars for a while."

I appreciated the significance of his teaching because I also once had, in an errant act of bravado and because I underrated natural forces, allowed a gust of wind to slam a green drake into my lip. It hung there for a while as fellow anglers feared pulling out the barbless bit of steel.

On that early morning, wading thigh-deep in the perfumed autumn light of Idaho's Clearwater River, the man showed me how to cast easily with a shorter stroke. He loaded the top of my loaner rod and shot its line halfway across the river, which was wide.

I didn't learn the snake roll despite his lesson. I toiled with my own version of a cast, one with a different name, days and weeks after the man was gone on his way to other rivers at least as famous as my home river. I continued to fish early, before work, mostly to cast under cover of darkness.

Much later in the season, I tucked the rod away without having caught a sea-run fish. My visits to the river had become less about catching and more about standing in the current to witness the first cold rays of sun flash on the water like a zephyr. What I learned on those mornings were small glorious puzzle pieces, moments of awe encountered briefly and tucked away before the current carried the rest downstream.

Education is like an arrowhead. Suffer the shards and you will create something to keep.

———————————

When Buzz came to the Clearwater River from Michigan he was immediately enthralled.

"It was the most incredible place I had ever seen," said Buzz, who moved on to guide on the Olympic Peninsula before returning to Idaho to teach anglers the subtleties of swinging flies to fish finning the Clearwater to their spawning grounds.

"It's not an easy river to catch steelhead in," Buzz likes to repeat. "It's a big river that doesn't give up its secrets easily."

Another man who has fished the river since the early 1970s, taught himself to cast a spey rod and learned how to hook steelhead from the best teacher, the river itself.

"I waded out wherever the water let me," Poppy Cummins said.

Those places are fewer now, the ones with access sans industry or no-trespassing signs. Their presence, though, makes fishing the big water feasible much of the time.

To learn the river's lessons you have to push against its current with wader-wrapped legs and the lock of your hips. You will stumble over its stone washes, slip across the bars of cobble watching for skinny rattlers that don't make much noise before they strike and be startled by the deer that clatter from the dry coolies. Cast your flies, the ones that leave a wake, and as best you can, swing them away from the opposite bank toward midstream.

Poppy likes a green skunk fly and if you visit him at the Red Shed, his fly shop outside of the river community of Peck, he'll give you a handful of flies and a leader. He will graciously tie them on for you and wish you good luck.

The former logging truck driver started fishing steelhead right here with a rod he built himself and dubbed the junkyard spey because of its many non-matching parts.

Poppy knows that learning to catch fish from shore with a long rod goes hand-in-hand with a certain river etiquette.

It's the same deference the man from San Francisco showed when he walked a quarter mile to ask how far I planned to fish.

Longtime spey caster Craig Lannigan, author, fly tier and river guardian often expounds on this chivalry once taken for granted but experienced only rarely these days.

The civility of bowing out is something he learned decades ago when the river was fished mostly from boats. When he found anglers waist deep in his favorite holes, he realized it was likely their favorite hole too. They, like Lannigan, preferred the quiet runs away from others and had hung their flag at the spot before he traipsed into it, making him the intruder.

Either way, he bowed to those wade fishermen who rose earlier than he did, only to swing a sparsely hackled fly into the bend by the leaning pine where the churning water curled over a trench as he stood on the road twisting his rod pieces together.

He waited his turn. He let others fish through and expected the same.

Mostly, he says, nothing is like it was when he started wade fishing with long rods in the 1970s.

"I've been low-holed so many times over the years, it's not good for my heart."

The code and the catch are equal parts of the same lesson. They are learned in the same flow.

Simple propriety contributes greatly to the knack of the sport on a river where the clear current of simplicity runs deep.

Respect the water and its fish, and show some gallantry, Lannigan says. Etiquette is the golden rule of spey rodding.

"We're all knee deep, wading the same stream," he says.

The Bull That Wouldn't Be

STREET CREEK—The bull elk stuck tight to the tangled growth and down trees of a ravine, snapping limbs, whining and chuckling out of sight and far enough below us that our approach would likely end in a bust.

Down there in the murky hollow where the bull hid, our pupils would dilate big as nickels as they adjusted to the lack of light. The vine maple and bramble cane laced with snaky rope grass would wrap around a hunter's legs, tangle the limbs of bows and shafts of arrows, whisper, "not so fast," and provide cover for the bull to spy anything sneaking in.

We sat in the duff on higher ground waiting for the nervous bull to come looking for us.

Up here, ponderosa pine mixed with clumps of sunny-slope ocean spray, elder and sumac, providing hiding spots for a hunter in otherwise open glades.

If the hesitant bull decided that our bugles and cow calls overstepped the line of civil discourse, and if the insults overcame his timidity, he would likely sneak up the draw of an old stream bed as he climbed the hill to check us out.

That was our hope, but we weren't absolutely banking on it.

"If he decides to visit us, I'll betcha money he'll sneak up the draw," one of us said somewhat half-heartedly as if testing the prognosis, having learned that elk aren't immune to surprises.

"How much?" was the reply.

Grass and duff-covered, the overgrown stream bed we thought the elk might traverse was quiet underfoot, thick with fallen needles and rotting leaves. It seemed the perfect route for an apprehensive bull to skulk in for a closer look at whatever intruder had invaded his stomping grounds.

I snuggled into a pocket of fir above the stream cut waiting for the bull to pass close enough to offer a target for my broadhead.

The decision was made after much deliberation that happened in a whirr of a few seconds.

At first, I was in the sloping meadow concealed behind the heft of a big ponderosa thinking that this bull, however demure, might just kick it up a notch and storm in to confront any comers.

But my mind started smoking because the bull had hidden apprehensively down there in the black hole for an hour or more while my efforts to slide down on my belly for a look left me dripping with sweat.

My noise and movements had quieted the animal as I busted twigs and debris under the soles of my ratty, Danner good-luck boots before climbing quietly back up the hill to where Jonas, my long-time hunting pal, had already become intimately acquainted with a camo-covered, big-bull yodeling tube.

Jonas is a man whose patience and calm in the face of inevitable defeat is countered by a sack of juju he carries on a string around his neck when he hunts with me. The bag of seasoning, small bones and Chiclets, I think, is supplemented by occasional chants, dances and eye rolls depending on the decisions I make in the heat of the moment.

These are the decisions that decide whether tags are cut or the ride home is filled with an awkward, hundred-yard silence:

"That was a nice bull."

"Yep."

"You prolly shoulda shot it."

"Yep."

I scrambled out of the holler and crawled back to where Jonas sat on a pile of pine cones stroking the bugle tube with a vacant look that said he had resigned himself to not being home in time for his kid's piano recital. Camouflaged and grease-painted, he sat in a patch of shade from a yellow pine as the estranged bull elk we assumed was a raghorn squealed and appealed for us to just go away.

When the bull stopped squealing we heard hooves stomping up the hill.

"Here he comes," Jonas said blankly, already aware that nothing good could happen from here forward.

I stumbled downhill toward the fat ponderosa pine in the

overgrown meadow and waited as thoughts ricocheted off the walls of my skull.

Over there is better!

No, over here!

Wait!

Maybe?

What?

Then I dove into the shady draw above the dry stream and hid behind a clump of fir, certain the bull elk would choose the flume as a safe shortcut to reach Jonas' now-furious bugles and squeals.

The six pointer — bigger than we had anticipated — clomped uphill like a climber knocking his toes into the dirt to get a better grip. He whistled with each breath and, fueled by adrenaline, focused on the place where he thought an adversary was messing with him, trying to run off with one of his cows.

There was a problem. After being teased and prodded, ridiculed maybe by what seemed to be an out-of-town boy frolicking with the neighborhood girls, our bull decided enough is enough. He had spent an hour at the bottom of the draw massaging his confidence into a honed fury. He shunned cover now and walked deliberately uphill through the open scab brush of the overgrown meadow and directly past the fat trunk of the pine that I had left a few minutes earlier.

As I watched from the shady draw above the dry stream the bull cut a wake through the September sunlight too far away for my arrow, but precisely on the margin of my sanity.

Jonas is a journalist and former roofer. There are times when he considers trading in his white collar job for the one he knew as a younger man. He longingly recalls dirty T-shirts, blistering suntans, tepid water bottles, fat paychecks and aching knees on a broiling incline three stories above residential subdivisions.

He has at times comforted himself with indecision instead of the rigidity required for resolution. During these moments of indulgence his future appears overly burdensome and worthy of deep reflection, which is where I come in. I help him recognize that life is a gamble and serendipity is just a sophisticated word for royal flush. Happenstance lets you soak up the scenery on your way to the ticket window.

It's not always like that, but the possibility allows for anticipation, the mother of hope, and faith, her freckled kid sister.

On this afternoon on a mountain in the Idaho elk woods, hunkered in the shade with a pile of elk calls, Jonas' seemingly sedate past met the carnal red-eyed rage of an animal determined.

The six-point elk found Jonas a hollow image of the bull he came to fight but better than nothing at all.

Jonas was reacquainted with a determination of his own. He believed he would be gouged and trampled, and hoped it wasn't so. Dropping the elk calls and his sense of aplomb, he rose to his feet and ran.

I lost track of the bull as it stomped uphill, but when

the cow calling, grunts and squeals with which Jonas had entertained himself stopped rather suddenly, I stood up.

There came a yell.

"He's right behind me!"

Galloping out from a knoll of trees on the ridge overhead was Jonas. The chestnut-antlered bull was close behind.

The scene was a dismal vaudeville, an old-time movie on frames of cracked and spliced film that caused the images to click haltingly — a man chased by an elk.

"What do I do?" Jonas yelled with an urgency I had not heard from him in a while.

He made brief stands behind trees and brush clumps, waving his arms, but the elk kept coming.

"Run this way!" I encouraged him.

It happened too fast to enjoy, but slow enough to reenact later as a simple pleasure.

What took place on that ridge, out of my sight, I cannot say, but Jonas finally emerged, sweating and shaking. He displayed the kind of emotional frailty usually reserved for the finish line of ultra marathons.

"Did you see that?" he asked as if wanting reassurance that he hadn't suffered an out of body experience.

"He was in our pocket," I said.

"I had to throw sticks to make him go away," Jonas said. "I thought I was going to die."

A man told me of shooting a raghorn bull at five yards that was being chased by a wolf. When he saw the hunter, the wolf made a somersault in its efforts to stop and reverse course, and the hunter let fly an arrow almost point blank that struck the bull behind a front leg, killing it.

"That was a memorable hunt," the man said.

Elk hunting in a drizzly fog one morning, another hunter's frustration won out after an hour of calling. The hunter stood and turned to see what he described as "the Hartford bull," standing calmly thirty feet behind him in the mist and the man almost exited his boots. When he pulled himself off the ground, the elk was gone as soundlessly as it had sneaked in.

During each archery elk hunting season, scads of hunters will meet their own opportunities and make do with their private successes or failures, naming them whatever they choose.

If they do not result in steaks in the freezer and another set of antlers hanging from the wood shed, the memory of a good elk hunt provides a different kind of nutrition.

It's reusable and often gets better with age.

Trout Hunting Lonely on the Joe

MARBLE CREEK — This is the river.

There are no blurring hatches.

It's too late in the season for the daily lookit what's flying.

It's almost November and the sunshine boys and girls
are gone, those fast-walking people in their bikini tops
and knee-length shorts and always the tan lines, slim slick
of sunglasses and flippy floppy sandals under summer's
wantonly endless sun.

The seasonal flyfishers too are home watching football.

Good thing.

Today is a mass of gray as if the low clouds want to press
the color from the landscape. Hidden are steep canyons and
the greenery of cedar and fir.

The tamaracks are still yellow. Some call it orange. It
means the late autumn storms haven't hit, puffing the
needles from branches and tossing raspy leaves from the
cottonwood trees.

Knock on wood.

She wears a red checked wool shirt with sleeves too long and a Montana Griz ball cap with a football logo. Her waders are sucked high above her chest. The water spools past leaving eddies behind her legs and the oblong rings disappear into the cold, blue-black that ripples away downstream like a sigh.

When she whips forward the LOOP fly rod its line spools out quietly and the fly lands at the edge of the run and any pickup truck driving by on the road has a rifle inside.

I'll bet.

There are few vehicles, though, and even fewer people standing in the river waist deep feeling the autumn push of current heavy and chilled against their legs.

It's elk hunting season in the mountainous valley and the hunting down here, in the cold moving confluence of time and water that pushes against rocks, undercut banks and scours subterranean trenches is good too, I'm told. So, we're hunting trout.

The river from Calder to Gold Creek is mostly devoid of anglers. Every so often a pickup, van, or SUV is nuzzled against a rock wall or tucked into a turnout above a trail that leads to the stream. These are the quiet pacifists of the rifle season, the Bachs of the classical scene, the string instruments played in the chamber with doors closed compared to the summer anglers' brass in the orchestra halls.

Late autumn anglers fish by themselves and the river welcomes their modesty, succinct casts and meditation.

From Falls Creek to Packsaddle, a wild stretch of white

and blue water usually filled with summer revelers, we count three vehicles.

The campsites are empty.

We drive below the bridge where the campers usually loll with ATVs and boom boxes blowing noise into the sky like bonfires, but any sign of celebration is gone. We rig up and move into the cold river like deer, casting and watching for movement under the surface but see none.

The low, concrete-colored sky mutes sound except what the current makes. We cast but catch nothing.

Soon, we're back in the rig heading east, upriver.

We stop to creep down a steep bank and splash into the water near Slate Creek, plying the flow but don't get a look. Farther upstream, near Packsaddle, we log a few takes, hold footlong, dripping fish, fat and lethargic. We slip them back into the current before climbing the bank and going for another drive.

She presses the lid off a beer and grins.

We lumber up Halfway Hill and down the other side passing a rig parked in a turnout and two solitary anglers a quarter of a mile apart who lean against the push of the river and we keep going.

At Tungsten Creek we park and slide down the bank by the culvert and walk downstream. A braid of the river joins the mainstem, a two-pronged current where a series of gravel bars make furrows and rills and the water splits and reunites.

A big stimulator imitates late-season caddis, those bugs fat as the thumbs of diesel mechanics.

We tie a length of line to the hook and add a copper nymph that will bounce near the bottom of the stream underneath the caddis imitation.

"If you can't catch them on the surface, use a dropper," a dentist long ago told me as I sat in his chair with my mouth pried open, and it's proven better than pulling teeth.

Use honey, your imagination, whatever works, someone else advised.

The fly floats along and drops over a shelf. Underneath it, the nymph cascades into a pool. There is a twitch and the stimulator is slurped south under the current. We set the hook. A cutthroat trout eventually is grabbed by the tail and lifted, dripping, up and out. It is red-sided and has a mouth like a can opener.

Wow, we say to ourselves, and the woman with the checked shirt casts again. The fish is released. There are more like it and we climb back up the bank and lean against the truck and twist off a beer top for our efforts and take turns with the cool golden liquid in the slim clear bottle. We consider the waning daylight, then load up and drive downstream.

Not far from the valley where moose often idle in spring, we stop, slide from the pickup's bench seat, and walk through the fallen leaves of silver cottonwoods. They rustle against our boots and she says she has to pee. There is a wait, then as before we make tracks in the gravel along the river and push out into the current where the water tugs.

A raven's bell call and the whoosh whoosh of wings mix with the far-off whine of a chainsaw. A thread of current whispers over a gravel bar. When we move we hear the wrinkle of our gear. Waders, chest pack, the zing zing of a reel stripping line as we cast, and then the line falling, leaving a worm-like squiggle on the river's surface.

The stimulator bobs along a bank in a run that's barely visible. It might be a foot deep from this vantage, but it could be deeper. The current weaves through a roof of overhanging buck brush, the kind that breeds bugs in summer. They clumsily drop into the water and are slurped by trout like spaghetti noodles in July.

But it's late fall and the stimulator bobs joyously on its elk hair body through gray light without a sound before it suddenly sinks.

Check that.

There is a cold, slow, swish and splash. The feel of a sizable fish as it struggles and lumbers against the taut line and witching stick of the fly rod.

"You're only using ten dollars of that hundred dollar rod," a guide once accurately advised.

We let the fly rod cursively bend as we reel the fish closer and grab it. It is long as a forearm with a shiny, spotted back and a faux, bloody red stripe under a jaw. Cutthroat. A deserved moniker. Its mouth gasps as if it wants air. We set it free and try again.

Watch this.

The line spools out and the elk hair fly sets on the surface in the narrow slit of a runout. A bead head nymph plops into the water along the bank like a coin dropped from a pocket.

The sound is muted as if heard through earmuffs. The day is a dull drum in which sounds, emphatic in other seasons, are whispered in confidence.

This time the floating fly drags the nymph away from the riverbank. The indicator bobs like a dinghy in an outgoing tide before it is slammed underwater.

Fish on!

This cutthroat trout is bigger than the last. We admire its colors, the red sides, orange and yellow gill covers.

It inspects us.

An amber eye with an obsidian pupil.

An unexpected ray of afternoon sun cuts through dull clouds and slicks the fish's sides. She takes a picture.

The trout is dropped into the current and immediately disappears against the river's golden bottom.

We walk through the leaves to the pickup truck and drive home.

Little Victories

HELLS GULCH — The coyote is an example.

He lies like a shadow in the low spot of the hay field, nose to tail. He curls where the warmth of the night mixes with the scent of whatever is coming or going, or what animal has come and gone.

The air down there where the coyote rests, barely moving and cool, is like water with dust on its surface film. It is a soft swirl of detritus and living and dead things, carapaces, feathers, the lint of a fawn decapitated last summer by the haybine, mice and voles, the warm duff of time and friction. The atoms of air all mix with the meh of living deer and the soft huff of elk that, last night, crossed the low ground. The aroma the coyote knows is a roadmap blended with echoing chirps of hoppers and crickets from yesterday, the spawn of ground squirrels asleep in the earth. The air, in its slow colloidal movement like a river's eddy, stirs hair, calcium and hay stubble, new grass that pokes and breathes and leans, frosty or dew-wet, toward autumn under fading stars. It strums the antennae of the coyote's whiskers.

From this vantage, the coyote can read the Sanskrit of his surroundings effortlessly with olfactory glands developed over thousands of years and if there's danger he will smell it before he sees it.

The approaching school bus sweeps its lights across the field and the white wash of headlamps bounces over swales where the coyote lies.

The small dog is there most September mornings supping the remaining eddy of warmth. He took the pullets last month, three of them, one at a time. I found them dismembered, feathers mostly and scaly feet in a knoll near the field. He ate the neighbor's cat, harried the pigs and tore the hide from the rump of a Targhee ewe before the herding dog chased him away. He sniffed the kibble dish of our pointers who silently eyed him from their kennels, too timid to counter their kin.

Scratching at the lawn's edge for voles, he urinated on the fence posts, jauntily zigzagged through the apple orchard and checked for afterbirth from the Limousin cow that bellered all night from across the road.

I don't begrudge him any of it, as I wake up this day and squint out the window and see his hump of fur and ears and bone in the dip of the hayfield in front of the house. He stretches as the first rays of sunlight slip through a crease of eastern mountains.

I tiptoe across the cold floor to the rifle on the table.

This is the dance we both know, the coyote and me. It is

the hunting dance. It is the eluding and returning-at-night-to-prey-on-livestock dance.

We accept each outcome with silent concession.

The rifle is loaded.

My daughter wakes up.

What? She asks, rubbing her eyes.

I put a finger to my lips.

Dad? She asks.

Coyote, I whisper.

"I want to see."

She wakes another sister and another who tumble from their beds wearing pajamas.

I have the rifle now in my hands as we stand near the window. We're in the shadow of the unlighted main room and I lead their eyes with my words to the low ground across the field by a strip of uncut hay where the coyote stands as a fuller light of morning arches golden in the treetops. Sunlight, like a rising tide, now rushes toward the field, quietly casting its brilliance through pine and poplar and over the hay stubble. Its frothy tip has not yet reached the small brush wolf.

That's what we, as boys, called coyotes and the words then alarmed me.

"Brush wolf."

I say it now and the girls, my daughters, sisters in elementary school, their hair like straw, feel the same wildness in the words.

The name recounts the untamed yip and howl that, in the dark, is an outlandish and eerie cacophony.

The spookiness of the neighborhood coyotes' wild, nighttime howls is tempered and forgotten as daylight approaches.

"I see it," one of them says. "It's right there."

The youngest of them drops a shoe on the wooden floor as rays of sunlight whisk night into a dustpan.

From across the field, the coyote hears the shoe strike the floor. So far out, a hundred yards maybe more, the wild dog cannot smell us, but it hears the thump.

He is a young dog, thick with autumn fur, the growl and bark of last night is a burr in his throat and the sound of the shoe on the yellow cedar makes him jump.

He is frighteningly alert.

Immediately he is all legs and his tail falls straight behind him like a lever. He leaps into the air and his legs whirl. It is as if he swallows large gulps of air with each lunge and the breathing fuels his forward momentum like a chugging engine.

I remember the words of my neighbor, Doc, the man on the steel seat of the McCormick FarmAll who told how, heading to town in his pickup one day in early summer, he saw a canid in my field when the hay was waist high. As a man who raises Targhees for the income that pays for his land, taxes, and the repairs for his tractor, he didn't hesitate to raise a .22 caliber from a seat scabbard. He leaned the rifle out the window and squeezed the trigger but the shot was low and the wild dog, already in full sprint, kicked his own dust over the dry dust the bullet made and was gone into the trees before

Doc rechambered and refocused the reticle. The brush wolf disappeared into a stand of tamarack along the creek.

And this coyote, the one we see, the girls and me, now races toward the same grove of trees.

I hurry across the floor and out the back door. It bumps against the jambs shivering the rusted screen. I kneel on the plank decking of the porch and lay the .257 Roberts on the frosty porch rail.

The barrel is pointed at a rise in the field where I expect the coyote to cross.

I wait for it, seventy-five yards away, to break into view for just a moment, a glimpse, and when the coyote reaches the swale I squeeze the trigger.

I kneel at the same place on the back deck where I shot the barn cat.

The cat, a family pet, foamed at the mouth when the girls were younger. It stood hissing in the driveway.

"Hydrophobee," one of my daughters said. "Just like Old Yeller."

The boom from a double-barrel scattergun made a smoking hole where the small, sick cat had been.

The daughter who said it stood then where now I'm kneeling, and like a young Travis in the Fred Gipson book, she reassured her sisters that a shotgun blast was necessary medicine for the young, sick cat, which likely had gotten a face full of antifreeze, not hydrophobia at all.

And now she watches from the window as the coyote bounds across the field into view and I point the barrel of the

Roberts rifle ahead of its lunge and the trigger snaps, and the dog disappears.

"You missed it, dad!" I hear a daughter yelp from inside.

The girls eagerly throw on sweatshirts, jackets and boots, and we walk out. We step across the frosty field. The gray edge of the morning has turned buttery yellow, but we still push our breath like wisps of fog ahead of our walking. The ground is crusted with frost. The girls wear rubber barn boots and wool barn jackets. The smallest one, just four years old, wants to see the coyote. It is one of the animals whose songs have lulled her to sleep and also kept her trembling awake.

Dark, those nights with the guttural howls and yips and keening. But it's light now.

We walk out.

And that is what I mean. That is an example. That is how it was and will no longer be because time jumps and skips and skitters across our conscience like a flat stone. It leaves the water and touches the sky's reflection and returns to the water farther out until it sinks and we stand, ankle deep, watching the rings pass over our feet.

It is just the passing of time, we say by way of explanation. Just time's tick-tock, moving calendar pages with our notes and reminders flipped and eventually replaced.

I skinned the coyote.

My daughters watched.

They stood in a circle around me. They touched its fur and said, soft.

As the others grew bored and went inside, one of them

remained. She asked about muscles and bones. About teeth and jaw and olfactory glands.

"Can I help, dad?" she asked.

She wore a red sweatshirt with an elementary school logo.

I gave her a small, sharp folding knife and she said, yeow.

"Do I cut here?" she asked. "What is this muscle?"

She is grown now, has a job and a car and college courses, but talks of it still.

"I remember everything, Dad," she says.

That was years ago.

Buck of a Lifetime

ST. MARIES — Samuel Fuller drives a lumber truck.

Back and forth, back and forth from the drying kilns to the plywood plant all day.

He brakes for traffic as he pulls the double or triple trailers loaded with fresh-cut fir and makes a wide arc at the four-way stop. He always smiles even at the drivers who have him shift down, stop and clutch.

He waves.

I'm Sam Fuller and I've lived here all my life.

He whistles. His radio crackles. Sam Fuller, that's me.

There are other drivers, but everyone knows Sam behind the wheel of the big green truck that makes the three-mile trip six times a day back and forth between the mill and the dryers. You can almost set a clock.

Last week, everyone knew Sam for another thing. He killed that massive buck.

"I have been meaning to do that for a while," he said.

There's a season in the Panhandle when the elk move from high timber to the deep brush draws where muzzleloader hunters seek them.

The occasion for the bugle is over.

Snow falls.

The cinderblock motel in town begins to fill.

"We got about twice what we had last year," said the owner. "I expect we'll double that again next season."

He's talking about trophy white-tailed deer hunters.

They come from the Great Plains, the Great Lakes or the North Woods to bag a buck like Sam's.

"They read about it in magazines," the motel owner said. "We've got some of the best late-season whitetail hunting in the West."

These out-of-state hunters get locked in. The idea of driving a few days to tramp public land west of the Rockies for a trophy buck begins to gnaw at them when outdoor publications print the deer forecasts, usually in August.

But the buzzing in their ears and the tugging at their hearts started the same time last year because a similar article told of North Idaho's hefty whitetails.

They pack their cars and make the three-day, thousand-mile trip to hunt mostly public land for a handful of days.

Sam traveled a half hour to get where he was going that snowy morning last week during the rutting season when the bucks chase does and seldom sleep or eat.

"I've hunted that particular area going on thirty years," said Sam. "I've taken probably a half dozen nice bucks out of there."

Those other deer, though, paled compared to this one.

That morning when he woke and sipped hot coffee from a ceramic cup in the half-dark kitchen of his house in one of the town's newer neighborhoods, he pulled on his woolen pants and he knew.

He had fueled up his pickup truck the day before.

He had a sandwich already made and would eat it on the way out of town.

His lab stayed on the dog bed by the coat closet and gave him a look without whining or carrying on.

"It was just one of those mornings when everything seemed right," he said.

He understood there would be no guarantees, and he didn't think of asking for any.

No quiet prayers. No rubbing a talisman or wearing a lucky hat. He didn't consider clicking the button to hear a favorite CD. He didn't even turn on the radio.

He simply packed the sandwich, thermos and the gun case that carried the same old 1960s model 30-06 he's carried for the better part of his adult life. He has talked himself out of a new rifle by believing he cannot afford one. Not one like this.

"The gun is aces. A nail driver. Still has the original barrel."

"A new one will cost me ten bills."

He bought a scope for a little over a hundred bucks in 1996 and screwed it on. It remains clear as Glockenspiel.

When he parked his pickup, he slipped the rifle from its zipper case and loaded one cartridge at a time, then slipped under the forest service gate, cradled the rifle and walked the road. He cut a few deer tracks in the gray morning and crouched to examine a set of much bigger tracks that joined the smaller ones.

It's not a long story.

He kept walking until he found the buck by following the tracks in the snow-covered gravel, maybe a half mile.

He stayed just far enough behind the deer to not scare them. He likely did this without knowing it, he said.

He didn't whistle. He didn't sing or talk to himself, at least not out loud.

The falling snow helped muffle any noise that may have come from him.

He followed the tracks until he saw the deer up ahead. They appeared to not notice Sam who now stood by a cut bank looking through the scope that straddled the action of the 1960s model 30-caliber.

"First thing I saw was the mass of the buck's antlers," he said.

Even through the falling snow he recognized the significance of this deer and felt himself shiver, something he had not done during a hunt since he was twelve.

He unlocked the rifle's safety mechanism with his thumb, heard it click and feared the sound would scare the deer.

As the small herd stopped and the buck turned sideways, Sam held his breath.

The scene, he recalled, was like a postcard. He exhaled and touched off a round a little too soon, he thought.

He may have flinched or moved.

The rifle jumped and the blast echoed in the valley,

bounced from the surrounding hills and was quieted by the falling snow. As the three does sprang up the road bank and disappeared into a strip of tall, snow-covered grass along a clump of firs the buck lurched too. It took three steps up the embankment and fell back into the road.

"I just stood there," Sam said. "I chambered another shell and just stood there thinking he'll get up and run away, but he didn't."

He saw blood in the snow where the deer had slid.

Then Sam walked carefully with his rifle drawn. When he reached the buck he touched an open eye with the muzzle of the 30-06 as he had been taught by his grandfather. It was a gesture he had not performed for decades, but he did it now. The eye stayed open, it didn't blink, and Sam put his mittened hands on the rack that measured almost as wide as his gun.

He wanted to shout but was afraid of the sound it would make.

Then he let loose.

"Woooo Hoooo," he yelled. It didn't come out as loudly as he anticipated.

He yelled again, this time louder.

From his right hand, he removed the shooting mitten with the finger flap and clutched an antler and again the cold girth of the walnut-colored bone seemed too much, like the taper of a baseball bat.

He stood on the logging road and looked around at the old clearcuts, grassy meadows and strips of standing timber filling with snow. The air smelled like wet smoke from slash piles smoldering somewhere upwind. He felt snowflakes strike his face and melt.

For miles, no one to hear me shout, he thought.

He drew his knife and carefully cut and caped. Steam gushed, warming his skin and despite the falling snow, blood dried on his hands.

He'll have the cape and antlers mounted. It was his wife's idea.

You'll never shoot another one like this, she said.

"It'll probably cost me ten bills," he said.

It's the buck of a lifetime, and why those hunters are packed into the cinderblock motel.

Winter

Bitumen and Leather Boots

He was a cargo kicker in Southeast Asia before he could find Vietnam on a map.

Riding those sweltering airwaves over the steaming jungles waiting for the signal, knocking open the doors of the Otter or other fixed wing, hooking the chutes like they teach the kids of the 101st, sliding the boxes across the floor of the fuselage to the windy opening, and then slinging them overboard, bang, bang, hoping not to hear the popping of ordnance from the big guns or the plinking of small arms fire against the plane's aluminum skin.

The round silken chutes fluttered and snapped and he hung his head out the door to watch the crates spin and swing to earth while thinking, "We sure as hell ain't in gawdam Montana anymore."

He learned to kick cargo after enlisting as a smokejumper in Maclean's hometown of Missoula, Montana, where he jumped out of airplanes for a different army called the U.S. Forest Service.

One day in college a man in a suit approached him and said, son, Uncle Sam could use a few like you.

It's better pay than fighting fire, the man assured. Safer too, he said. Come see the world.

So he hooked up.

Next thing he was a college kid in blue jeans on sticky asphalt or red dirt tarmacs in Southeast Asia eating rice and cabbage, orange and brown sauces that burned his mouth and bowels. He earned the title loadmaster, which meant he made damn sure the boxes he dropped into the highland villages didn't break on impact, busting the stocks of the wooden carbines, M1 Garands, Korean and Russian AKs, or spilling ammo, 7.62 mm, and 5.56, the kind that bounces around inside before making an exit hole the size of a coffee cup.

He dropped chickens and goats, crates of military fatigues, radios, plastic conduit for water systems, pumps, farm tools and medical supplies.

That's where he met Fylo Buck.

It was the boots Fylo wore that asked for an explanation.

Despite the wind that flapped around inside the snub nosed de Havilland like a wet towel, he sweated in the cargo hold staring at his own ten-inch White's leather smokejumper boots that made his feet blister and stink. He looked across the payload piled in the aisle and at the other guy sitting in a web sling seat.

He looked French.

Cold. Lean. Unflinching.

He wore a green beret and carried a short machine gun.

This guy looked hard and dripped asshole, he thought, but strapped to his big feet were White's smokejumpers too, with ten-inch shafts.

"Hey," he yelled over the engine noise that sounded like a wind tunnel. "Where'd you get the White's, man?!"

The guy wearing the green beanie and leather boots with the tall tops and block heels briefly stared at him, then looked away.

"Where'd you get the motherfuggin White's, man?!"

He yelled again.

"I don't know what the hell you're talking about," the man yelled back.

He learned later that Fylo was a snake eater, what they called U.S. Special Forces guerilla soldiers before anyone knew what they were, or where.

When the cargo dropped, Fylo Buck jumped out of the plane behind it.

Good-bye McCall, Idaho. Hello Montagnards.

There's a certain fraternity in boots.

As a boot guy, that story, told to me once at the Fort Wainwright smokejumper base in Fairbanks where Fylo Buck spent his retirement years, stuck with me.

The guy who told it also worked at the base and years later reunited with Fylo. He was a boot guy as well.

He and Fylo became close friends after having spent months together in short-runway planes scuttling through swirling mist in Southeast Asia, or above it, before that part of the world blew up.

The whole crew at Fort Wainwright were Bureau of Land Management smokejumpers and boot dudes who shopped around and tried out a variety of leather footwear, learning the nuances of hook and eye, block heels and spring heels. They expounded on the virtues of high tops, low tops or why screw-in caulks sucked and how the glory days of logging — and firefighting too — rested on a particular type of boot.

Boots are important to people who make their living on their feet.

When I was eighteen I bought a British motorcycle and a pair of Carolina engineer boots that got stepped out in a couple of seasons.

I went through two pairs of the black and buckled footwear, spending them on pavement across the Great Divide and although the motorcycle, a 1971 Triumph TR6, didn't change, the boots did.

It was Carolinas, Durangos, Dingos until I settled on Wescos because I wore their logging shoes in the woods where I worked. They were affordable and didn't give me a squeak heel.

Last winter she gave me a pair of Wolverines.

I said, baby, if you want to buy me something for Christmas go to Goodwill and get me a pair of carpenter boots, so I don't get snow in my socks.

It was a suggestion over coffee and under the kind of gray skies that make your toes cold.

She presented me with a brand new set of Gore-tex lined

leather boots with a hard toe and ten-inch tops with canvas on the outside.

I said, no, baby, I can't accept these.

Try them, she said.

Naw, really, this is a big commitment, I said.

Don't let it worry you, she said.

It did of course worry me, but that didn't matter to her.

She looked all over town for them and found them at a place in Post Falls.

Take them back, I said.

Not a chance, she replied with that look that let me know she had done an unselfish act and I needed to graciously cast aside jaundice.

Even when she left I wore them.

Told myself not to.

Said I no longer should, but wore them anyhow. Every day. They began to take on an odor.

A logger came into my newspaper office in winter wearing the same damn boots.

"Best I ever had," he said.

The snow that January piled so high I'd wade knee-deep to climb up and into the cold cab of my pickup truck.

But I never once got snow in my socks.

That's all a boot guy can ask.

Mule Bear, Oinky and Me

Mule Bear wasn't known for his ferocity, stubbornness or ability to bounce like a deer uphill through the pinon forests of the Rocky Mountain states.

He acquired this term of endearment because he spent most of his time in his mother's basement eating processed food and watching nature shows on cable.

A latchkey kid whose dad ran a marina and whose mother raised three children while keeping a full-time job and a comfortable home in one of the town's upscale neighborhoods, Mule Bear's existence was mostly sedate.

When we played pool in his basement Saturday afternoons as teenagers he enlightened us with the learning he got from the other side of a TV tray watching Western Wild, or Predators of the Pioneers for hours while enjoying bowls of pizza pockets and soft drinks sipped through swirly straws.

Grizzlies were unable to scale trees because their claws stuck in the bark, he expounded after an episode of Wild West

Bruins. Their movement up or down a tree trunk is impotent as a sabertooth in a tar pit.

"They stick to a tree like gorilla glue," he hooted.

We looked at him with suspicion.

Mule Bear also deemed mountain blacktailed deer the most majestic two-toed cud chewers on the continent and promised that one day, like the brawny horseback guides of squeaky saddle lore, he too would spend weeks in the mountains glassing for the magnificent, drop-tined creatures.

These musings were significant because to us, a gang of boys who often dragged Mule Bear from his basement to do fun stuff outside, they were the foundations of Mule Bear's moniker.

A softish, affable boy and nominal sidekick, Mule Bear grew into a football lineman by the seventh grade and towered above his peers, prompting his mother to bedeck him with oversize clothes to keep ahead of his growing. To his pals, he became a walking billboard of sorts.

If one of us owned a tousled coiffure it became a "Mule Bear cut." Baggy jeans from a downtown merchant were "Mule Bear slacks," and a slice of gas station pizza or a high-carb, low-value beef burrito was invariably "Mule Bear food."

Muley, as we called him for short, preferred button-front flannel shirts with sleeves too short because they shrunk in the wash, showing his wrists. His boots were Irish Setters and in the rare moments when we walked him into the woods after upland game birds, he carried a Wingmaster shotgun that his father purchased as a gift.

In part because of his college-aged brother's fraternity ties, Muley knew his way around liquor cabinets with the learned ease of a union boss or someone often left unattended with the likes of single malts and an array of Frankfort bourbons.

And because his older brother, when he wasn't in college, worked for pops on the docks with the globetrotters who visited from Florida in summer, cannabis, the kind that floats your teeth, and big tri-hulls became Mule Bear's passions.

Home grown bud with seeds that popped like bacon could be purchased by the handful at the River Diner, a local biker bar, but Muley's was the immaculate and moldy herb that scented a room like shower soap, silk bathrobes and leather house shoes without the slobber of a curly coated retriever.

Nuthead got his name because he was tough as a nut and, if he grabbed hold on the wrestling mat it required a wrench to loosen him. Blaze was a fullback and fast. Boone had a boy beard at a young age and liked to hunt squirrels for the pot. Buggy was an oversized boy who bought a Harley Davidson motorcycle in high school and longed for a showgirl and a sidecar. Conan, because he read The Barbarian comic series and knew the best scenes by heart.

I became Bart. We had Boggsy, and Honer — variations on a last name. Slim, Nellie and the Polack brothers, one and two, belonged to our troupe. Otto because his last name was Lilienthal and we foresaw a crash, and there was Hammer and Hard On and Kooch, names that arose from various athletic or other accomplishments. Jehosaphat had the rust-colored hair of his Scottish ancestry, was squirrely with enough of the Yosemite Sam demeanor to earn the nickname that later became Jolly, because he smiled a lot without saying much.

Other peers went by Haybale and Zep and Oinky for reasons forgotten or misplaced, but the Mule Bear moniker still turns the heads of the many who knew him.

Once, while a group of us escapaded in a mid-1970s model Buick LeSabre, enjoying the scenery and the spirits from his mother's liquor cabinet, Muley asked why we called him that.

There was a shrug.

"Just 'cuz," someone offered, and Mule Bear seemed fine with it.

Mule Bear's acceptance of the moniker seemed to liberate him and allowed for more thorough libations, nature channel viewing and Hungry Man meals with a TV dinner tray set up downstairs like a holy water font.

The lack of a fighting spirit resulted in Muley losing his position on the offensive line of the junior varsity team. He grew into his father's dungarees, went to work for his dad, and when we saw him later a much larger Mule Bear often cajoled us with the latest libations and exotic smokes.

He became a marina man, inheriting his father's business, while we — the rest of the hackneyed nicknamers — made ends meet and eventually dispersed with the forthwith of a flock of winter buntings.

A while back we were informed that Mule Bear had died.

"Dangit," someone said. "That's not good."

Loquacity is still too dressed up for our modest beginnings.

"How'd he die?" The inevitable question.

"Shoot. Muley weighed four hunnert-plus pounds," was the answer.

We lost touch, a lot of us because that's what happens when years downshift or speed up. It's nothing to pine over. One's sense of self-worth or matriculation seems overly important and something we lacked early on. Its deficiency kept us together.

Whether Muley got a chance to chase blacktailed deer in the Rockies isn't documented. He may or may not have learned that a grizzly's inability to climb trees is a misconception.

We want to remember Muley with the reverence his grace deserved and for the sensitivity with which he thrust forward in life.

In the mountains, where mule deer clatter on the rocks under towering yellow pines, I sometimes lift up his spirit without saying why.

I just do it, because.

Hair on the Floor, End of An Era

SANDPOINT — Larry Barton is in the chair and Clarence Davis is waiting for a haircut while raindrops splat against the big window facing the street that reflects everything in the barbershop like a mirror.

Larry wears an apron around his neck and Clarence waits patiently on an old sofa under the full body mount of a cougar attached to the wall near the ceiling.

The cat straddles a limb of yellow pine twice, once on the wall and again, mirrored in the window glass along with flashes of traffic and people walking outside holding umbrellas.

Just over Clarence's head, and below the grimacing cougar, hangs a black and white photograph from a 1950's fishing expedition. The men and women in the picture smile as they hoist a string of oversize Gerrard rainbow trout.

On the shop's walls are deer heads too, and mounted trout and bass. A four-foot pike with a string of lures attached to its mouth grins at customers.

Outside, cars and trucks rumble past. They rattle the floor when a man wearing a ball cap walks into the shop rings the bell attached to the jamb and says, "How's it going?"

Mike Winslow, whose shop this is, and who stands concentrating with a comb and scissors keeps clipping.

"Old and ugly, how about you?" Winslow retorts.

The man with the ball cap chuckles and digs in his pockets for a reply and Mike follows up like a right hand behind a jab when the glove is in your face.

"Didn't expect me to tell you the truth, did you?" Winslow says reaching for a hand mirror.

In this shop on Sandpoint's main drag, where the decor includes antique wooden fishing plugs — one hundred or more — and steel fishing spoons, also a hundred or more hanging alongside photographs from past angling and hunting days in Bonner and Boundary counties, the mostly men who place their feet on the scraps of carpet that pretend to be rugs, practice their oral history.

Not all of them wait for haircuts. Transients are welcomed and treated pro bono to the embellished accounts that pass as history, however refurbished.

The wooden fishing plugs, decorations now, were used to troll for the lake's still-plentiful and record-size Gerrard rainbow trout and each is inscribed with the name of the person who brought it to Mike to hang on the barbershop's wall in the decades since the 1960s when Sandpoint was considered a sportsmen's mecca.

One of the plugs is large as a banana and painted white.

Rick Topp's name is on it.

Whoever carved it did a fine job, Winslow says.

"He thought the bigger the plug, the bigger the fish."

When Topp trolled it behind his boat for Lake Pend Oreille's rainbows, "It was ripping line off the reel so fast, he had to put both thumbs on the bail to keep it from tearing all the line out," Winslow says.

Bill Garvey's plug is red and white.

"We could tell Bill Garvey stories all day," Winslow says, and Larry and Clarence shake their heads like they know something no one else does.

"You could even print some of them," Davis says.

Davis, 79, once a local boxing coach who sent several youngsters to national tournaments, has been coming to this shop for a haircut for so many years he can't put a number on it.

"I remember when you didn't have gray hair, and you had a lot of it," Winslow needles.

Davis blushes.

"That must have been a while ago," he says.

Winslow has nicknames for many of his clients. He calls Bill Fournier "Swivelneck," for the way he craned at a pretty passerby one summer's day long ago.

"I was just trying to see what kind of Bible she was carrying," Fournier cracks. "I was a lot younger then."

The man with the ball cap asks Mike if it is true that after fifty years on Sandpoint's main street, Winslow has plans to retire.

"Anybody want to buy a barbershop?" Winslow asks between clips.

He isn't serious about getting a buyer.

"They got to have the proper credentials," he says. "They got to be uglier than me, and cut hair as bad as me."

Winslow's tenure as the town's barber is noteworthy. He's been "cutting and lying" on the town's main drag for fifty years including forty one years in his own shop and before that, for nine years in the 1960s he barbered at Vern's down the street.

"They ought to put you on display," Barton says.

Winslow assures Barton he doesn't like the limelight or the police line-up, but retirement should be alright. He'll golf more and spend summers in his T-Bird with the top down.

He should have retired years ago, he says.

"It shows you how long you have to work if you invest in booze and broads instead of stocks and bonds."

Winslow's shop is a museum of stories sporting the artifacts from a lost generation of North Idaho outdoorsmen and women. The local historical society has asked for some of the relics, but the stories likely will not be passed along as prolifically as they are, day in and day out, in this shop where the clippers buzz and the scissors snip.

"There is a lot of history on that wall," Winslow says.

This week he'll remove the heavy glass barber pole outside by the door. The original one was busted with a beer bottle on a Saturday night when the town was a wild hootenanny.

The only solace, he says, "There was a lot of blood mixed with the glass on the sidewalk."

He'll probably take the pole home. Maybe use it as a mantlepiece, or sell it.

He has contacted the men and women whose relics grace his walls.

Many cannot be returned.

"A lot of good friends aren't fishing anymore," he says.

An unusual silence follows.

He keeps clipping.

My son says driving to Lewiston is too far to travel for a haircut.

He says this in response to the grousing I do about the local shops that have closed, and the ones that are too new, too full, or ask too much for a haircut.

When he talks about driving to Lewiston, my son refers to Sam's shop on Main Street. It adjoins the community policing station that closed after Bill Clinton left the White House and the money stopped. It is a couple storefronts down from a sex shop with a name reminiscent of lingerie.

Just as Mike Winslow, Sam has cut hair in a small storefront on the main drag behind a spinning barber pole for as long as most people along the Snake and Clearwater rivers can remember.

Many of Sam's clients are cops, soldiers from the National Guard, coaches, kids and retirees.

Each Tuesday morning for years Sam flipped the sign

and unlocked the door a few minutes before regular
hours to let in Mr. Allen, who came to town for his weekly
haircut and to talk about growing up a Nez Perce Indian
in the homeland of his forebears. As Mr. Allen sat under
a white apron looking at himself in the mirror across
from the barber chair, he told stories of the olden days
catching lampreys in Asotin Creek and eating them.
About the annual pilgrimage to pick berries as a boy, and
about traveling on foot across rattlesnake country from
Cottonwood Creek to the salmon traps. Mr. Allen owned a
mechanic shop and when he retired, he drove around the
country in a well-tuned sedan visiting family and friends.
He kept a garden, mostly so the deer could eat, and every
Tuesday morning Mr. Allen, at 84, was the first one to sit in
Sam's barber chair where he got his flat top trimmed until
one day he no longer did.

Sam stopped the clippers.

"We lost him," he said, as I stared at myself in the
mirror across from the chair in his shop with an apron
around my neck.

Sam, who still plays guitar in an all-string band, talks
about fishing the Imnaha and Malad rivers, about barbering
for a year in the North Idaho logging town of St. Maries
way back when, and how, down along the confluence by the
railroad bridge spanning the St. Maries River, he occasionally
caught pike.

If you ask, he'll tell you about the local Lewiston tonks
where he played music for a half-century.

"It was a boomtown then," he says.

My son who is twelve knows Sam from the stories I tell about his shop.

Down there, it's usually a short wait because Sam doesn't ask how to cut your hair, he just does it. And quickly.

"Who's next?" he barks between drinks of water from a plastic bottle as he waits for a client to pop out of one of the folding chairs that line the wall by the coat rack.

A broad selection of outdoor magazines spill from the table sometimes onto the floor and patrons pick them up, throw a foreleg over a knee and page through them to pass the time.

When Sam sweeps the hair from around the barber chair and says who's next, one of them will drop a magazine, walk across the creaking floor to sink into the warm upholstery — seafoam green — and wait for the flutter of the apron and the humming of the clippers.

The haircut is twelve bucks and takes ten minutes, and in that time you learn about taverns, long gone, former police sergeants, hooligans, establishments where beer and burger once cost a buck, and how to shoot an elk.

I got a haircut recently in a Coeur d'Alene salon with walls devoid of trophy mounts. They were replaced by TVs, shampoo, a half hour of primping and the process was professional.

I left a few dollars for a tip.

It's not something Sam would expect because tips make him uncomfortable.

"The price is what it is," he says.

Leave an extra dollar and, half embarrassed, Sam will offer something in return.

"You finish reading that magazine? Go ahead and take it. There's no end to them."

There is an end to those old shops and when Sam turns the sign on his door for good, who knows where I'll threaten to go for a no-nonsense ten-minute cut, and the education you only get in old barbershops.

Right Out of the Box

I think we remember knives.

We grew up with them as an idea, aware of their danger and value as tools.

Small folders with bone or wooden handles. Others were vinyl, the color of blood or mahogany with shining bolsters and polished pins.

Our knives were valuable to cut and ply and maybe whittle. They sharpened a stick, peeled the coat off a golf ball — a dangerous endeavor — or were flicked open-bladed into the dirt with a wrist movement that was also learned. We cut line, if there was spare line to cut, carved initials into the thin bark of birch or poplar and opened and closed the blades of these folding knives, always wary of their sharpness and the pain we feared a deep cut would bring before we piled them into a front pant pocket where they made their own warmth.

The earliest knife I remember is one my dad bought at a store that had the false front of Western movies. Behind big glass windows a saddle was displayed, lariats, western and farm jackets and the name Zetterberg was painted in golden block letters as if for a bank.

The doors were double and their brass handles, suspect. The thumb latch was irascible, so my dad worked it, and the bell as the door swung open made a sound sleigh-like even in summer.

Inside, the place smelled of leather and wheel grease for farm tractors, dry wood from the walls and floor, and the tung oil that made the deck shine.

We were there for a knife and my dad said it to the man, old I knew then, and I know now, the son or grandson of the original owner and the place, a going concern since 1912, long after the county was formed and named for the Ojibway word "snake."

It was better known for its pine and logging railroads and then its corn.

That's how the schoolbooks relayed the county's history.

The man wore denim overalls like a farm worker but without the odor of livestock, and he led us, slightly back bent and thick-fingered, to a display case with a glass top and small hinges and hasps. I chose an electrician's knife, no longer sure why, and my dad asked, was I certain?

I nodded yes.

It had two blades, one speartip and one screwdriver flat, and a ring on the end that was later lost. The bigger, flat blade closed on my finger once and cut painlessly deep and made it bleed and I sucked on the wound, wrapped it in tissue paper and masking tape until the bleeding stopped.

I told no one.

At ten, a blunder such as the one that caused the cut was not something you advertised to them who had the authority to take away the knife until you were older, or more ready.

A kid three years my senior ran with a knife and fell. The blind eye from then on was gray and didn't move much and when it did, it looked in a direction where nothing was.

I learned not to do that.

I used my knife to skin the squirrels I shot. Sold the tails to the Mepps lure company to garnish their spinners and I ate the squirrel's scant meat the way my mom had me cook it.

A couple years later I was sure I needed another knife to better pelt the muskrats I trapped at a pond a half mile behind the house where I hiked before school. The knife was named Muskrat Skinner and I saved my allowance and squirrel cash to buy it. For almost a decade it was part of my daily attire, until it was misplaced, which is the fate of most pocket knives.

I was gifted a Buck belt knife as a teenager, and inherited a Puma skinner with a beveled, leathered sheath. I lost both on the hill behind the house while hunting deer.

I searched in vain for days, sometimes on my knees.

An Uncle Henry pocket knife purchased at the local hardware store was lost once. The company sent me another for free. I still have it.

I switched to Gerber later because of their stocky handles that were easy to grip while skinning deer with short, wide blades that didn't puncture the gut. The stout tools used fair steel and I was reminded once how the company assured customers their knives were razor sharp straight from the factory.

A man in a bar reiterated this fact late one night near closing time.

It was a rainy, dark winter on the coast when I found myself in a near-empty tavern surrounded by heathens who wanted payback, I'm not certain for what.

The bartender had disappeared and I was nursing a beer when the three men surrounded me and showed their sheath knives.

They threatened me by sticking the sharp points into the wooden bar top loudly, and said the end of my time on this earth was fast approaching, unless ... Unless what?

They didn't explain.

The door swung open and like a scene in a Spaghetti Western, a gaunt man, balding, nursing a limp entered the establishment and walked slowly in our direction through a wash of neon from the beer signs, dragging a heel.

He sidled past my antagonists to the bar, sat beside me and asked how things were.

Then reached into his pocket, nodded politely to the three bearded and toothless buffoons who had surrounded me and, producing an orange-handled Gerber, snapped open the blade so the light from behind the bar flashed on its steel lending an air of ferocity.

"Sally," he said, simultaneously addressing each of the drunken and long-haired wombats, "This is a Gerber Vulcan.

It has a four-and-a-half-inch blade, and a non-slip grip."

He paused and looked wearily at the men who leaned now precariously like bowling pins.

"And it's sharp, right out of the box."

The three men were quizzical at first, then perplexed, then tilted away from us, shared a look, sheathed their knives and left the tavern as the thin, balding man with the limp slid to the end by the bell and rang it.

The commotion prompted the bartender to emerge from the can, or wherever he had earlier disappeared.

He brought two beers from the floor cooler and I remained beholden to the man with the limp, to his words, and his Gerber.

My culture was rife with blades. Rapala knives were either long and thin for fileting pike, or they had short blades for panfish. They came in a leather sheath with a loop but were kept in the tackle box instead of attached to a belt. Sometimes they hung on a hook in the boathouse by a dirty window veiled with spider webs. Victorinox had the Swiss seal and were useful for more than bloodletting.

Over the years I bought Boker, Green River, Case and Solingen steel knives. A Hartkopf I later misplaced was purchased in a shop on Munich's south side where the trains stopped before heading to Italy.

Damascus steel was something I considered, but let go of, and I have the names of local knife makers, and small-time crafters who stamp, forge and grind skinning knives from

Priest Lake to Lewiston and I intend to follow up.

I haven't owned a SOG or Kershaw, but once, coming out of Iraq, a U.S. Marine who had spent his tour in Fallujah kept his Ka-Bar despite the jaundiced comportment of customs officials in Kuwait who took his M16 magazines and my Swiss Army Spartan with its spear tip broken from misuse.

"Write it off as a combat loss," the Marine said of losing the metal magazines he'd carried on missions in the Anbar Province.

His fixed blade was hidden in a boot.

"At least they didn't find my Ka-Bar."

I last saw him walking with his kevlar helmet and brown SAPI vest slung over a shoulder heading into a crowd at the Amsterdam airport that opened to let him through.

I sat down in a lounge overlooking the tarmac to sip coffee served in a small ceramic cup and to remove the Uncle Henry folding knife from my sock.

My Blue Heaven

CLARKIA — It's way out where few people go.

The roads that niptuck the Clearwater National Forest in the St. Joe River drainage head to destinations like Orphan Point, Freeze Out and Indian Dip.

They are two tracks that end in the clouds with names that depict the loneliness of their venture, and whose origins are forgotten.

Dunce Cap Rock, Mulligan Point, Devil's Eyebrow.

Buried in winter the roads are scab rock washouts that serve as streambeds in spring and their maintenance logs aren't found in Forest Service archives.

The backcountry is so far from human habitation that one July, when he went to retrieve the gear he left in winter, the trail was blocked with a tepee.

The men in the shelter had cut trees to prevent passage. Sawed them off. The tops of the sawed poles hung in the limbs of standing pine like deadfalls. Beyond them, the interloper's cone-shaped canvas abode dripped dew.

No one gets past here, they said, as he approached.

I do, he replied, so get that canvas contraption out of my way.

They obliged.

The men grew marijuana on that federal land where only a satellite could find them. Small blips and orange holes like pupils dilating, and above them in the sickle sky, the Milky Way was their nightlight.

They were right, though, he said. Not another soul out there. One hundred and fifty miles from anywhere with a certain steepness that the sun only sometimes cracked. Mostly the ridges were clotted with the deep shade of subalpine fir, tamarack and knotty pine.

That was before GPS.

He learned the land the old-fashioned way with a contour map, bed roll and lots of legs.

Most people don't mess with this land because it asks too much of them, he said. They are stuck to their computer screens like magnets on a refrigerator. They come out here sometimes in the fall and snorkel around for elk and maybe mule deer and rush back to their camp trailers with guns drawn against predators when the sun falls into the Western hemisphere. They dig out a Hungry Man, tune in the satellite for the TV sets inside their RVs and are home in time for work on Monday.

They don't stretch themselves very far. They don't know the howl of wolves up their backside, and the snapping of tinder under hooves or the fitful sleep in a bed of boughs. The woods are silent for days except for the animal noises — some you only guess their origin. Some of them you learn: The scream of a cat, the chuckle of a wolverine, a bat chirping under loose bark or the scuttling crawl of a porcupine up a tree.

The weekend woodsmen don't travel far from their campfire rings because their imaginations won't allow it.

I used to love it out there in the high country, he said.

Walk with all your gear on your back. No burden. Just hoist it and tighten your boots. Cinch a belly strap. Guns and hard tack, bullets and canteens of water. The liquid blue sky, hard as a Japanese glass buoy.

It's a long walk. One foot in front of the other and you keep going for days.

In winter, it's snowshoes. Snow so deep you're carrying pounds with every step. After a mile of that, exhaustion is the jester on your back.

"It's steeper than the back of your neck," the legendary Dooley Cramp once said.

And it is.

You learn pretty fast.

One winter, he watched a bull moose with antlers like a cowcatcher come down a draw with snow piling on its shoulders. The double palm bull was like a gopher pushing the stuff over his haunches tunneling down through it.

That was before the wolves.

Few animals survive in the high country in winter anymore. When the conditions beckon the predators walk on top of the snow, and the elk and moose, the drop-tine mule deer — the real goliaths that once lived up high in winter — are tunneled five feet down, looking at predator paws when they come. They are furrowed in their trails and the wolves are executioners. There's nothing to it. It's like an archeological dig when the snow peels off layer by layer in summer.

That's what he said.

Hooves, horns, teeth and jawbones.

The scant bone marrow sucked out like spaghetti.

"Those animals were run hard, and got too tired to get out."

He took a snow cat up, back then, and saw the wolves lope in its tracks. The first one decades ago was white.

"I thought it was a dog," he said. "What's a dog doing way the heck up here?"

They kept coming after that.

Big black-tailed deer, the ones with antlers that could fill the bed of a pickup truck, left the high country as the wolves came on. Soon wolf packs populated most of the outback drainages, he said.

"Everything changed after that."

He lost a couple wives while he was up there by himself for weeks at a time.

He won't say it but in the house where he lives among the guns and traps and photographs that go way back, and the antlers, skulls and hides, in the house with the big garden out back, vegetables, and flowers of all kinds, he has a lot of memories on the walls. They are pictures of family, friends, ex-wives.

The women couldn't stand being alone so long, he said. They fell away like the miles under his tracks.

Adios, they said. Sayonara. Sorry, but ...

They left notes with magnets on his refrigerator, in his boots, or rolled up in the ceramic cylinders of his coffee cups.

"Goodbye."

Sometimes, he says — he lets out a laugh that makes his lips jump — I was gone for weeks under that cold sky with camp smoke curling into the stars and me in my bedroll with my boots on.

"No one knew if I was still pushing breath."

Children. He has those. Grown now. A new wife.

In winter he fishes the Sea of Cortez. He stays out of the backcountry.

But he recalls those earlier years with fondness, his hands folded as his body bends to the tailgate of a pickup truck. He would barrel out of Clarkia or Avery on a snow cat with a bearing toward Montana, the Larkins, or My Blue Heaven. He cut trail over the tops of trees because the snow was deep enough, always looking for animal tracks as the azure, momentous sky pressed against his shoulders.

The sky was blue as glass by daylight. At night it was the hooves of a Pegasus pounding. Translucent, it baptized him, blessed him with spangled specks of star fall.

My Dad once asked me, "Son, where the heck are you going? I need to know just in case."

I told him, "Dad, there's no point in telling you because if anything happens, no one will find me, anyhow.'"

Not until spring, or when some hunter by chance kicked his mossy bones years later.

"I had angels with me," he said. "Or, lotsa luck."

The maps are in his head.

"I blazed a lot of trail," he says.

He imagines those trails still exist and the maps, he believes, remain veined in his memory.

There was this lake in the Larkins that he would drop into after shooting a mountain goat and packing it through the trees to let the meat cool. He would follow the trail he carved to this little lake like a single pearl at the bottom of a cirque. He doesn't know if he can find the lake anymore.

It's still out there, he is certain of that. It is beyond the radio noise, so far from the orange skull cap that cities wear at night, beyond the muffle of consciousness in a rick of land where pine martens bark and skitter and fishers growl.

It's beyond Indian Dip and Sawtooth Saddle. Somewhere south of Surveyor's Ridge.

He leans over the tailgate of a pickup truck with his hands folded, his hair gray and the slit of a bifocal in his lenses.

"I loved being out there," he smiles.

Every night was Christmas Eve, he says. Every morning was a gift framed with foggy breath and each day was as radiant as the pictures from a satellite dish.

"We leave pieces of ourselves in those places," he says.

They are atomized, muted, swirling like aurora borealis through the fans of lodgepole pine or mountain spruce.

Remnants of songs, scent, the quiet dissonance of our existence. They are glitter snow or pollen spores, breeze-blown, that bore the duff like a seed bank.

What's left are nanoparticles scattered under the vast rolling ocean of his blue heaven.

Time, Toils and Tollbom

SANDPOINT — Ward Tollbom has painted an owl.

It is a small owl and the watercolor seeps around the perimeter of the painting.

He says to come look, so I do.

He says this because he has not matted my prints.

It has been weeks.

When I walk into his Hen's Tooth Studio on Sandpoint's First Avenue next to Dann Hall's photography shop of exquisite black and whites and the color photo Dann shot at the Vancouver Games of the guy with the Go Canada! shirt zipping his pants in the Port-a-Potty complex, Ward says, hey.

He says they are not finished.

It's amazing how busy I am, he says.

Ward is 60 but looks like a guy in middle age who has spent a lot of time eating fish.

He has that Norwegian glow like he dreams of sea air and eats sea air and doesn't spend too much time worrying about the oil rigs dotting the North Atlantic.

He is too busy enjoying the small things in front of him and painting their likenesses on canvas.

Come look, he says. So I do.

It could be a screech owl, or a barred owl or a burrowing owl.

It is meticulously depicted, almost photographic.

I don't ask which kind of owl it is because both Ward and I have biology in us, the study of natural things, and I should know the species without asking, so I do not ask.

He attended the University of Idaho dangling the idea of a science major but instead turned his eye for detail into art.

When he was at the university in Moscow many years ago, he longed for the lake, tall trees and the mountains of the panhandle, so he painted them.

"It's pretty dreary down there," he says. "Especially in winter. All brown and gray."

One of the first things he painted after learning perspective and how to pen a field of wheat was Sandpoint's City Beach, its white sand, sailboats and magnificent vistas.

He did it from memory.

Next he painted the barns along the Pend Oreille River, as he remembered them, and the forested mountains where he and his father chased deer.

His dad was a one-legged grocer. Raised a family that way.

His wooden leg hangs from the wall in Ward's shop next to the pictures of deer and moose that he and his family killed and ate, and the antler mounts.

When Ward has a lousy day he considers the leg, the leather straps, the pain of it.

"He did it on one leg," he says. "I can do it on two."

There's a fishing lure, too, still packaged, hanging from a nail on a post in his studio.

It is large, metallic and treble hooked.

It is a version of the lure used to catch the many mackinaw that Ward and Boots Reynolds hoisted into their boat one day more than a decade ago on Lake Pend Oreille.

They made a hundred fifty bucks apiece on the bounty paid by the fisheries department.

"Better than going to work," Ward says. "Those days are gone, I think."

In its effort to kill the predators of kokanee, a type of landlocked sockeye salmon, the state fisheries doled out dollars to commercial and regular anglers to harvest and generally wage an all-out war on lake trout and big rainbows in Pend Oreille. By gobbling the sockeye and almost depleting the population, these top-tier predators nearly toppled the lake's entire manufactured fishery.

The bounty worked, and it helped rebound the population of sockeye — also called silvers or bluebacks — the backbone of the lake's food chain.

Ward wants to catch a big rainbow trout again. The Gerrard stock. The kind that catapults into the air and wraps fishing line around the outboard and generally whoops it up.

Mackinaws, he says, "run deep a few times and shake their head," before you reel them in. They don't provide the excitement of a twenty-pound Gerrard.

"Lookit this," he says, and I admire it.

It is the owl painting.

The bird is small, slate gray, and barred. Its feathers are almost tactile. Individual barbules want to move in the air of your breath.

Its eyes look into your eyes.

A sharp beak is stout as a bent nail. The landscape around the bird is silent.

I hold the picture as if it is the owl itself.

I don't ask what kind because it would betray the distance I have laid between my past.

A decade ago, I would have said its name, but now I no longer have it.

"That's beautiful," I say, instead.

Ward is happy.

He doesn't get to paint often anymore.

"It's amazing how busy I am," he says.

I'll return for the prints another time, I tell him. There's no hurry.

Spring

SOMEPLACE, IDAHO

Well Balanced Shotgun

A well-balanced shotgun is the one you gently remove from the rack and throw to your shoulder in the gun aisle of a hardware store in Cut Bank, Montana, swiftly aligning the sites on the barrel with the rocket-like doves or cannon-shot chukar that make a deep dive over the condiment aisle into what you envision to be a rimrock canyon as a splash of wind blows your hair back.

You feel it immediately.

The weightlessness of the shotgun. Not the wind. Unless there's a breeze through the door that has been stopped open with a wooden wedge carved on a day less busy than this morning.

You swing the gun briskly as the birds top the counter and disappear into a wall with a poster advertising a cotillion.

You feel the butt end of the twelve-gauge gun smoothly snug your shoulder as wide-eyed you peer down the length of the twenty-eight-inch barrel at the make-believe birds wheeling toward a make-believe pattern from an unspent shotshell.

A make-believe spray of one and a quarter ounce, number six shot looks a lot like the specks of dust in a shaft of sunlight through a high window.

As if magically the trigger is pressed against a finger and you don't say bang. You don't consider it. The moment, this brief glorious anomaly of grabbing the gun, hoisting it in an instant, and having it point exactly where it should, is a thrill like newfound verse.

It is the opening notes of presto. Better yet, prestissimo!

The store's other patrons include a man wearing a Western shirt massaging an elk bugle to ascertain its necessity in the seat pouch of his pickup truck, the store clerk feather dusting boxes of Havahart raccoon traps, the young mom whose pig-tailed daughter wears shorts and a sun-bleached T-shirt as she considers a mallard or wigeon decoy for Father's Day. They don't pay you any mind.

They fail to flinch or scatter as you swing the over-under gun.

Mostly they are not more aware of your presence than of the ice-cream cooler or the gumball machine, the newspaper rack, or the broom by the door.

They don't hear or see the birds that roused you and made the gun in your arms swing so effortlessly.

The hometown store is a place where neighbors of this High-Line community gather routinely when they opt against purchasing from a catalog, or their internet connection is kaput.

They nod to the clerk, say hello, and maybe call him by name. Or they don't make eye contact at all, ever since the news that he, you know, with that Mrs. Johnson, or that he paddled his dog in public, or was caught in a ditch with a bottle of moonshine, even though it has been years ago.

Small-town life is a hex and a pool of forgiveness eventually.

From the broken shoulder of the highway as you drove through town you recognized immediately the mercantile was old-style and not a refurbished hipster or avant-garde establishment. The store with its creaking floor and ceiling fan, hand-tied trout flies in a glass case, brand new, wood-handled mops, freshly-stocked wax toilet rings, cantaloupe, tomato plants and Mepps fishing spinners all in the same room with a pile of hand tools, shotguns, thirty-caliber shells, and camouflage dog beds drew you off the pavement like a sign for lemon meringue pie.

(Two for one today because they were baked on Thursday.)

You stopped in the gravel lot to watch a boy in a Resistol Denison hat and Sunday clothing — the white shirt buttoned at the top and Wrangler jeans cardboard straight with a denim accordion above each boot — being admonished by his mother. She made him dig with an index finger a wad of snuff from a lower lip and drop it in the gravel, then spit, before returning to the cafe next door.

From the wall behind the counter with the ancient cash register, elk, pronghorn, black and whitetailed deer heads eye customers rigidly, but with an air of sanctimony.

This is the one, you say to yourself.

About the shotgun, not the store.

This is the one I must have.

But you're three hundred miles from home on the rise of the Rocky Mountain front carrying in a billfold the cash you must squeeze for gasoline and jalapeno corn dogs and whatever sustenance is required to make the trek through the snow-spired mountains to the river valley far to the west where you live.

So despite the billfold bulge, what merchants call cash in hand, you concede to fall back on that which you usually fall back on.

Air and noodles, sometimes, or just vistas and the knowledge that what you want today will take a backseat until tomorrow.

And besides, you already own a well-balanced shotgun.

You are certain of this.

It's true the gun back home doesn't have a name recited in a century-worth of outdoor magazines or advertisements stuffed as insulation between the walls of old farmhouses to keep the knifeblade of winter wind from prying in. Its name is not written in gold letters on the box of cartridges you have tossed on the bench seat of a pickup truck, your grandfather's, dad's or your own, since you were fifteen.

The gun back home has its own flair, and an orange dot site for reasons yet undiscovered.

Its action is engraved with squiggles and curlicues not fowl, upland birds or pointing dogs. The engravings on your shotgun are machine-made. The lack of the ornate isn't dwelled upon because the gun's schnabel is fine as a pheasant's beak, its forearm is checked — although not by hand — and the stock is walnut.

The Turkish gun, bought at a big box store whose name will not be uttered, is well-balanced, and proven so.

The clerk with the duster realizes you have in your hand the shotgun he has been eager to ring up since Christmas, but you smile and tell him, "Sorry bub."

You know neither his name nor his past.

Nice gun, you say. I may on another occasion stop by for it.

You both realize this is a ridiculous sentiment.

You both understand the value of the gun and lust for its contours without hearing the firing pin click, or the bang of a shell in its tube.

"Want me to set it aside for you?" the clerk asks like pitching a penny over a shoulder.

You shake your head.

That's a well-balanced gun, you say to yourself as you drive away, heading west.

It's almost noon, you should be home in six hours.

Then you recall your own less-expensive over and under gun, the one you carried effortlessly as your pointer held and you knocked a brace of pheasants from the cloudless sky.

You saw your dog hesitate and then drag back both birds at once.

You remember the clear coat of the gun's walnut and how you slipped and dented it on a gnarl of lava rock while chasing chukars, but managed to drop a bird on that particularly windy day high above a desert river.

Indeed, it's a well-balanced shotgun too, you tell yourself.

Didn't it ride just fine on the roof of your car where you forgot it as you headed home after a hunt last season?

People on the highway pointed, but you haughtily paid them no mind.

You were full of yourself with a pointing dog asleep on the floor mat, and the birds in the back already dressed, their plumage a courtly regalia.

Filled your limit of China hens, dint'cha? Huffed up, you were. And deservingly so.

You were proud, feeling a bit regal, all of which was offset by the well-balanced gun that rode on the roof of your car like a squirrel on a wakeboard. Motorists pointed, honked, tried to make eye contact then shook their heads as they sped away.

A little humility makes the soul big. It shows that even a small budget has room for a gun that withstands the dippiness of its owner.

The gun stayed on the car roof where you found it when you returned to your maple-lined neighborhood.

You got out of the car, saw the gun balancing profoundly on rails of the luggage rack, and immediately looked around.

Your neighbors were all inside behind closed doors, so nobody noticed.

You realized the implausibility of what had passed.

And it immediately pleased you to own such a symmetrical thing that could balance for forty miles on the roof of a car traveling sixty miles per hour without falling and shattering on the pavement and maybe being minced under the many wheels of a cow truck.

Sometimes it takes a well-balanced shotgun to cover the surfeit of one's transgressions.

Hoisting a Coeur d'Alene Brew

PRICHARD — Meet Andy and Scott.

They sit on lawn chairs on the shoulder of the Coeur d'Alene River Road.

It's a sunny morning, the first of a long weekend and the beginning of flip-flop season. The floaters here are thick as sour cream on an Idaho spud.

Traffic is buzzing, automobile license plates are out-of-state and upper echelon Panhandle.

Andy and Scott are fishermen from somewhere around Spokane who ply the water with hair flies, bead heads, wooly buggers and other things which will remain undisclosed.

Everyone has a secret enticement that can be slipped from a vest pocket when neighboring anglers are tipping a brew. It can be tied on and cast without eyebrows lifting or tongues trembling like aspen leaves.

Today, the only breeze is from the traffic that scuttles wrappers alongside the road.

Andy and Scott are alongside the river road raising canned beers at passing cars and laughing.

Motorists wave and honk.

Those guys are plain having fun.

The men and women behind steering wheels who drive past all abuzz on creme de menthe or Black Rifle espresso, gas it on the straight runs, veer around barefoot inner tubers who pick their way over pebbles on the gravel shoulders carrying their inflated rubber donuts like bumpers.

The drivers point their chrome in the direction of weekend haunts they mapped during work days when they planned a getaway and now hope there's a place to park in this amalgam of shirtless humanity.

Andy and Scott aren't concerned.

Not much at this point.

They parked in a turnout several hours ago when the temperature was still chill and the sun was barely over the Bitterroots. They slipped down a trail wearing felt-soled fishing shoes and waders and vests to a shady pool they know.

It's a fishing hole everyone knows.

"It's a good spot," they say.

The two men fished this morning and lost a bunch of the wild cutthroat trout that flashed in the slow-moving water like dervishes.

They drowned their woolies, nymphs and stones in the cold water, casting and drifting.

Trying a little bit of everything.

"Don't know if it was my knots, or if my tippet was too small," Andy says, rattling off a few excuses we all consider when having a good time is more important than pulling in fish.

"But I broke a bunch off," he grins.

They caught some trout too and let them go, so the fishing evened out.

Then they climbed from the water, slogged up the trail to their pickup truck leaving wet boot prints behind. They removed their gear right down to a pair of shirts and tank tops, pulled out folding chairs and popped the top off some cold ones. They plopped themselves down right there at the intersection where the road heads east to Montana, the Sprague Pole or Prichard.

There's a tavern nearby and shade, in case either is deemed urgent.

With their bare feet dangling flip flops and resting on drugstore coolers filled with ice and their ball caps turned back, neither Andy nor Scott express a sense of urgency.

Downriver at the Golden Beaver a fishing guide, huffed up and casting for listeners explains his theory on the Spey rod to anyone within earshot.

"Casting it is like painting the ceiling," he says.

It is lunchtime and the place is packed.

Spey rodding is the physical equivalent of Vivaldi, the guide loudly moans. It is van Gogh's Starry Night without the color and the missing ear.

"You get that by chucking spoons," he cajoles.

Listeners sense he has told these stories before. They whiff of the circus tent with silk screen tulips and a hint of Van Morrison's wild abandon.

The sport who has paid the guide a lot of money to fish an overfished fishery sips a Keystone Light — Andy and Scott call it river beer — waits for the waitress to bring his burger and fries, and listens courteously while smiling politely. His eyes are blank as if he's lost in the sanctity of moving water while the guide, a man possessing the acuity of a fried potato, pontificates.

I order a steak with blue cheese and listen too, and wonder why we afford someone so much patience who takes people's money to bore them and watch them fish.

Upriver Andy and Scott are still laughing. They have hung up their rods for the day, thrown their fly vests knotted with streamers and hooks and indicators into the beds of their pickup truck. Their legs are bare and their shoulders and cheeks are red from the sun.

They paid no one to come here and now listen only to each other's lilting banter.

They wear tattoos and grins like watermelon slices and they don't hear Vivaldi or think about van Gogh.

It's Saturday. There are fish in the river with flotillas of tubers and half racks of beer, the traffic on the river road is a procession made up of exhaust and radio noise and the air is filled with the marvelous quicksilver of their own making.

There is nothing else they could want right now.

That Turkey Hunt

PANHANDLE COUNTY — We passed through town
and crossed the river, then veered and bumped from the
pavement onto the old Civilian Conservation Corps road to
the camp where the men three generations ago had lived
at night while spending their days in the surrounding
mountains. Their job was to uproot currant and gooseberry
ribes that acted as a host to the fungus that killed the white
pine — a valuable commodity.

We followed the train tracks that had once hauled the
timber and the mining to the big lake, the embankment was a
trail now for bicycles.

We jumped rills and tunneled through trees then
skipped up a lean road along the edge of the mountain
gaining elevation.

It was too early in the morning for sun, but birds, robins
and warblers, the skittish phoebes, warm-weather bluebirds
and juncos whistled and crooned under the still-gray wash of

sky and when we stopped, a sheeny coin-color of light brushed the landscape.

We slammed the gobble call, then listened.

Hear that?

The question was a quick turn of the head or a finger, pointing.

"Sounds like it's across the river." This, we low-toned as if the bird, a quarter mile away, could hear us.

"Or, it's in that draw, a ways back."

Morning sounds are fanned by breezes, mellowed by moving water, and tossed around in the rock-shelled bandstand of canyons.

We loaded up again into the small, all-wheel-drive family car, letting the doors slam in a cadence of empty soup cans. The tires spit rocks as we headed higher into the hills.

Eventually, we turned back.

The balsamroot and syringa blooms and the perfume of cottonwoods mixed with the first sunlight like a slick of seasoned butter.

We backed up on the narrow road as we had learned long ago driving dump trucks loaded with shot rock for the logging highways like this one. We would push the tailgate into the embankment, face the cliff, crank the steering wheel then breathe, dump the clutch, shift and accelerate when the front wheels again struck the road ruts.

This morning, we dropped to an elevation that seemed more conducive to bagging a tom turkey.

Crossing the river, we followed the same routine on

another logging road until we pinpointed a Merriam's on land
that was not fenced or posted.

When we believed a tom was within reach, we carried
the lumbering twelve gauge guns, the camo vests loaded
with shells — needing only one apiece — and face painted,
we climbed a deer and elk trail sideways on a slope
that had been logged a few years earlier to preserve the
historical forest.

The western yellow pine, also known as ponderosa, that
grows on south-facing hillsides in North Idaho's sandy soils
makes due with limited rainfall especially in summer. This
is where the great fires start, on southern aspects overgrown
with brush and trees that don't belong and have been
cultivated or allowed to grow because the burns that test the
ponderosas have been mostly quenched, eradicated, removed
from the system. When a fire does ignite in the unmanaged
tangle, it becomes an urgent problem mitigated only with gobs
of taxpayer dollars.

For this reason foresters first harvest the fir, spruce and
hemlock leaving the indigenous and always graceful, thick-
barked pine to keep the fuel-source low. Any fires ignited
here must crawl up the slopes like sticky slugs looking for
something to burn, instead of howling and kicking like horses
with their tails aflame.

The low-crawling burns massage the forest floor
preparing it for purple-flowered meadowsweet, ninebark and
chokecherries. They irrigate the needle-covered duff where
ground beetles skitter, moths flit and grubs grope, seasoning

the soil for fescue, wheatgrass and elk sedge. Gobblers graze these forests in the spirit of Jurassic omnivores.

When we aren't here, we long to hunt and sit with our backs against trees as the sun throws shadows under the cast of clouds like remastered Fleetwood Mac, egging us to sleep.

We are here today though, with our backs against a trunk while our peers in town frequent offices clearing paper jams and waiting on the coffee pot.

They may rue their circumstance, who knows, but we grin at ours.

This makes us happy lumber. We are camouflage-colored logs and lumps of slash. We are limbs dropped in a winter storm angled against a tree. We are stones and mounds of grass, well-armed.

When gobblers come, we look natural. We close our mouths to hide our teeth and raise our guns.

On this day, far from any mega town, we spoke turkey with purrs and yelps.

We scratched slate calls, copper pots, the ever-available box call made by people's hands in West Virginia. Our mouth reeds whistled.

There was no reason for a quick putt-putt, the spitting after-smoke of apprehension or alarm. Instead the turkeys we soothed with our fluent banter eased up to our decoys unawares. They danced for our rubber-feathered mannikins. Their waddles blazed blue as nuclear waste.

The early spring grass wasn't high enough to cover our shoes, but lush and green, certainly. Few flies buzzed. On a fire-scarred hillside across a canyon deer went looking for a bed.

Purple shooting stars, dainty flowers that appear like tiny cranes, tipped their beaks toward the ground. Fairy slippers, also small and fragile as mist, bubbled in the shade.

A single elk, then two, three and four grazed toward the shadows of a tree line.

She pointed at them.

See that?

One particular tom, brazen in his investigative need to bust our cover, made a beeline in our direction as others strutted near our decoys.

There were two shots.

The halcyon morning effervescent as soft drinks, became in an instant a rumble of cross fire. Two booming shells exploded as wings raised duff like sweeping brooms.

Fleeing birds tucked tails as they ran, sailed over road banks, flapped their wings over treetops. The banging of the guns echoed down a creek bed toward the river.

With the return of quiet, we gave each other a thumbs-up across a swath of sun-dappled grass. Then we rose to our feet like earth coming to life. We grinned again, ejecting shells from smoking breaches, pocketing them. We walked down the slope over the new grass to where two toms, their legs kicking, their maws mawing, lay in the soft, green road bed.

We collected the decoys, rolled and stuffed them into our bird vests with boonie hats and face masks.

Gutting the turkeys, leaving their offal for the coyotes,

ravens and beetles, the twin Merriam's were hoisted incongruously over shoulders, wings fanning our backs like shields, spurs biting the palms of our hands.

On the mile hike to the car we giggled at the astonishing beauty of the morning.

Faces streaked with grease paint, black lines over cheek bones, greens daubed on chins, noses and foreheads, we were the alien battlers of spring.

Having traversed a mountain pass, leaving our homes and warm beds in the city, we found another life as bird hunters.

A worthy spring endeavor.

Back there where neon blinked and traffic howled we might as well be cardboard-boxed like cereal.

Out here, as champions of a moment, heroes of the high-five, curators of the curious and wisened procurers of protein, we reclaimed that ancient solace others pay a shrink to find.

Pondering Spring Pike

COUGAR BAY — When the bobber moves, light a cigarette and smoke it. Crack a can of soda, or a beer if you have one, and when the cigarette is done and the beer is empty go ahead and set the hook.

That is what old timers tell Jordan Smith of Fins and Feathers Tackle Shop and Guide Service in Coeur d'Alene, the lake city's old-timey and iconic bait and lure shop on the once bustling East Sherman Avenue that is starting to bustle again.

Smith doesn't question the wisdom or the tales of seasoned, Great Northern Pike anglers who chase the lake's shallow water monsters each spring.

"Waiting for a few minutes before setting the hook is a real thing these guys do," Smith says, standing behind the counter in a T-shirt and ballcap as others sit around on stools nodding the way people do when they have heard something many times and have little to add to the paradigm.

The rain outside is an ice-worm-like drizzle that melts

dirty snowbanks. But since the avenue on the town's east side has gotten new attention from the city, the snow on East Sherman is already cleared and hauled off, so there is just the spring rain puddling water on the pavement, mirroring the sky and making outside aromatic.

Smith continues. His knowledge of area fishing is encyclopedic. His dad started the shop almost forty years ago while Smith, who is gaunt, unshaven and always enthusiastic in a subdued way, grew up with slime on his shoes and his hands welted by the dorsal fins of spiny rays.

Not setting the hook immediately when a fishing bobber submerges or begins to move, leaving a wake, appears improbable at first, he says.

"Right?"

The idea of angling, afterall, is to hook fish.

There is a method to this pattern of seeming madness, however, the men on the stools and Smith muse.

What follows is a pause heavy with the doldrums of the gray spring morning.

Cruising spring pike, Smith continues, will grab a dead herring or smelt that has been hooked on two trebles and hangs under a bobber that an angler has cast from shore to the edge of a weed bed. There are no weeds this time of year, but the beds and weed lines are remembered from last year. The dead bait sinks to the bottom and lays there like a day drinker at a rock concert. A pike, smelling pity and lifelessness, rolls up to the glass-eyed minnow and makes a quick grab with his jaws like a crackhead for a money bag. This is when the bobber jiggles. Old 'cuda face may be hooked but only gently. Because the bait has not resisted, the lumbering pickerel mouths it before he begins to chomp, and carries it away.

At this point of the story the bobber cuts a wake on the topwater. It is observed by an angler who is halfway through a can of moon juice and who has snuffed a cigarette under the sole of a rubber boot.

Scenarios vary.

The pike may swim with the bait to eat it elsewhere. Or, as Smith adds while others listen and nod ...

"If he's not hooked, ol' big tooth might drop the bait before coming back to pick it up again."

If the pike grabs the bait a second time, he will find a spot to idle and luxuriate as he chews and gullets his spoils, Smith assures his audience.

This statement, elicited from the counter in the middle of the room — the epicenter of the Fins and Feathers shop — is followed by another pause, pregnant as a bowl of guppies.

"Just watch the bobber and rely on your experience and intuition," Smith says and the men sitting on stools around the counter nod sullenly. "It takes a lot of patience."

But it ain't brain surgery.

"Might make you lose your mind," one of the men declares.

Dave Smothers of Post Falls hadn't considered idling at the counter of Fins and Feathers the fine, drizzly spring day he hooked a twenty eight-pound pike that measured forty five-inches long, a few pounds shy of the record book. He had planned to drive to a northern bay and with the patience that old timers save for spring pike fishing he would skewer a dead herring with twin trebles, one in the head and another behind the dorsal fin and hang the bait at the end of a long, steel leader. He would cast the contraption into the lake like a bolo and settle in for hours of bobber watching.

When his bobber ran that morning, cutting a wake, he figured the bait was carried by what he thought might be a hammer handle — a smallish pike, skinny with a big, toothy head. He watched for a while, like old timers do, before setting the hook. Soon he realized whatever was out there in the cold murk had some muscle.

"I knew it was big," Smothers said.

Big as a jackhammer.

He fought it for a while, feared losing it, landed it and although he doesn't keep most of the pike he catches, he decided to haul this particular fish home and have it mounted for his wall.

"Fish that big don't come around very often," Smothers said.

He looks forward to seeing a laminated version of the slough shark with shining eyes, its speckled and lean bulldozer body whirling, caught in a moment, motionless, in his living room.

Smothers began pike fishing years ago after retiring from a company that installs elevators in residential homes like the multi-storied cottages that hang from the hillsides along the shore of Lake Coeur d'Alene.

He considers spring pike fishing the best of all his outdoor endeavors.

"I bring a lawn chair and read a book," Smothers said. "I'll sit eight or ten hours a day, once or twice a week."

It snowed his first time chasing pike years ago. He sat through the squall in the pickup near a boat launch with his son watching a big bobber floating over the edge of what, in summer, is a flourishing bed of water weeds. The bobber was attached to a line that, about eight feet down, was secured to a leader and a pair of trebles buried in a dead herring. When the bobber jiggled and headed out to deeper water like a buoy in a rip tide, Smothers learned it wasn't called a "bite," but a "run."

"You watch the bobber take off, and you wait a good five minutes," he said.

He didn't have beer and he doesn't smoke, so he meditated on the Zen of the thing.

The words meditation, or Zen, didn't crowd his mind. He was anxious instead.

"We sat back and watched it go," he said.

Pike anglers, the ones who actively pursue the pastime are a secretive batch of modern berserkers who sit a lot, get cold, think about things once deemed forgotten while watching stuff — birds, dock planking, lawn chairs — float past in the rising water of spring. Because of the occasional floodwaters, they prefer a spring with a hard and deep mountain snowpack.

When mountain snow depth is above average in March and nighttime temperatures stay well below freezing, it prevents lake levels from rising too quickly. When runoff is slow, the spring pike fishing season is extended by a couple of weeks or more.

It is difficult to fish pike from a flooded shore, Smothers said.

Smothers' wall-hanger made a few deep runs, tugged and jolted and sought refuge in a jungle gym of piling from an old log mooring, but didn't break off.

That is because Smothers exploits a forty five-pound braided line to his advantage.

"There's a good chance they will wrap around something," he said.

It took him fifteen minutes to land the fish.

Smothers has caught many pike in the twenty-pound range and smaller. He releases most of them.

When the lake water warms and the pike spawning cycle transitions into a summer ambush and gorge fest, the solitary predators begin to attack moving lures. Smothers is among a small bunch of pike anglers who are not enticed to throw spoons or spinners over emerging weed beds when the season changes.

He likes the cold reticence of spring fishing.

"You're mostly out there by yourself," he said.

He prefers to hunker with insulated waders, boots and a book on knots, or a mini-series. And he religiously observes the method of old-time anglers.

When his bobber, after floating for hours, suddenly sinks, pops up, sinks again, then rises and begins to move, he watches it go.

His heart may start beating faster, but he calms it, looks at his watch and hangs tight.

All the action he can muster is just a few minutes away.

High and Tighty Gawd Aw Mighty

Hoo yah!

"High and tight please."

You could not see it in his eyes, but the barber on that
steaming, sultry day in that air-conditioned shop on that
shady street somewhere between Spokane and the western
front of the Bitterroot Mountains remembered a little
something from his days in the service.

"Sure then," he said, as over the years he learned to say
instead of the "Yessir!" he shouted as a kid toeing the blue line.

He slowly lifted the clippers from their place in a drawer
and the coily electric chord followed them into the fluorescent
room like a serpent.

I looked up from a hunting magazine.

No one else did.

We were eight to the wall facing three barber chairs
in a shop where aye-aye crewcuts seemed the norm,
but when the kid said high and tight like he meant

business like he was about to walk to an interview at the bricklayer's union, something inside me said you gotta see this.

I watched the stooped barber with his gray sideburns, the green and blue tattoos staining the thin arms that poked from a starched white shirt, click a button on the clippers with a thumb and away he went.

Every now and again he would turn the chair so the kid could catch a glimpse in the spotless mirror that spanned the wall under a stuffed largemouth bass, one big steelhead trout and a sign that implored, "Love It or Leave It."

Secured to the mirror's edge were "Nixon Now" and Carter lapel pins. A red, white and blue Reagan campaign button poked from a cork board that also lobbied for two Bushes and a Clinton. An Obama button, baby blue with a soft rush of red, stuck into the tongue and groove near a "Make America Great Again" bumper sticker that rallied from behind a jar of plastic combs hiding a "Ford in '76" button.

From somewhere under the blast of the sports channel on a couple of TVs showing baseball games in different time zones, I could hear Johnny Cash sing, "Sunday Morning Sidewalk."

The haircut didn't take long.

When the clippers quit buzzing and the floor was littered with what were once shoulder-length curls, the kid in the barber chair rolled his eyes to the ceiling as if he expected to find a lock on his forehead, but there was none.

Just a small dollop of hair graced the crown of his head like swag for a rumpus room.

The rest was neat as sidewalls.

With a small brush the barber cleaned the clippers like an umpire as the kid dug in his pockets for a bill.

The scenario reminded me of the blue tarp we once rigged between trees to keep out the coastal rain. We'd pull a greasy power cord, all of its forty feet, from the shop to take turns in the big wooden swivel chair we carried out from the kitchen, and gave each other buzz cuts. The next day on the crew bus that carried us to the logging job, we all looked different, but with the same haircut.

That was a couple of decades ago. I won't make that mistake again, I thought.

It's like going to an Eddie Bauer store to buy the shirt you saw on the mannequin and realizing too late that instead of looking like the guy in the catalog, you're Al Bundy in a Speedo.

I had come for a trim, just to take the stragglers off. I had places to be, a business proposal and some fine people to wow. My briefcase was tucked between my wingtips on the floor and my T-shirt was tucked tight at my waist.

My pleated slacks, tie and collar stays were the staid fashion of the day.

The kid, though, after collecting himself and paying the barber, didn't look too bad with the little carpet sample on his head.

He crossed the floor of the shop on his way to the door, his hand swiping his newly-groomed pate. As he turned the knob to go outside, he swiveled his head, nodded, and let summer's heat pillow in.

When it closed, the door struck a sturdy little bell that cried ting-a-ling.

The barber with the starched shirt and blue tattoos set aside the broom he used to push the hair on the floor into a pile and gruffed, "Next!" — a little too loudly, I thought.

I put down the magazine and left the briefcase under my chair.

With a scaly arm sporting bristly steel hairs and standing slightly hunched under the crisp white smock, the barber spun the chair for me to sit.

"What'll it be?" he asked.

On one of the TVs leaning into the room over the mounted bass and the glistening steelhead, an infielder bobbled a double play. Announcers coughed and chortled as the crowd noise rose an octave and the rest of the customers in the barbershop barely raised a brow. Their noses were pointed at pages in the magazines they held. All of them seemed settled on the comfort of a crewcut, same as last time and the time before that. Good enough for the girls we go out with. Good enough for the chicken sandwich special at the neighborhood's last corner cafe. And for their Fairlanes, Silverados, Sunbirds, for the sweet honey tree, and the Briggs and Stratton twenty-six-inch power mowers in their neatly-swept garages.

With a sideways glance at the barber and one eye on the door, I raised a hand to point at the kid who just left.

"One of those," I said.

"High and tight?"

The barber clicked the clippers.

"Sure then," he said, softly adding a "Hooyah," as if it were an afterthought.

And away we went.

Turkey Talking Is A Family Tradition

Leaving the toilet seat up, the window shades down, or eating the last half of a donut left in a box, family customs can be as motley as a carnival crew.

I know a woman who reads the newspaper every morning standing in the kitchen while the coffee pot perks.

"My dad taught us to do that."

There's no room for excuses if you stay informed, she says without the slightest wag of a finger.

This spring I pulled my mentor hat from a box of mismatched mittens, snarled fly line and hunting vests with broken zippers. The bucket hat is camouflage-colored, purchased at a yard sale during a trip through North Dakota.

I found a caked tin of face paint and striped my cheeks in headhunter fashion. Then, wearing the hat and grinning like a cartoon cat, I woke my son from his deep sleep under posters of Michael Jordan and recon marines.

"What's up?" he yawned.

"The woods are calling," I warbled, and hauled us both into the forest an hour away to sleep under a tree.

It's a family tradition, I explained.

Don't worry about the bears, hungry from crawling out of a hole where they have tarried most of the winter without a bite to eat, or the long-tailed mountain lions or the ratty-fur wolves.

Just grab a stump, or a thick yellow pine for a back rest, dig a small pit in the duff like a bucket seat and doze easily.

I'll wake you if anything happens, I told him.

A man I know in Superior, Montana, was a pretty good tree sleeper but he did it in the fall during the elk hunting season. He would shimmy up the side of a mountain in the dark, find a spot where he thought to find elk at sun up, and then drop off to sleep. Sometimes he awoke to give a bleat from his cow call.

He did this for years with some success until waking one morning in a patch of brushy timber surrounded by wolves.

They had come for a meal and he had enticed them with an elk call.

The incident made him jittery.

"Three of them, five yards away, and all I had was my bow," he grimaced.

It didn't keep him from sleeping outside again, but he takes more care when considering a hunting spot.

During the spring turkey season getting in the woods early to hear the birds come off the roost is a good way to locate a flock.

It takes a few trips to the boonies, past farm fields, grazing cows, the slow crawl of smoke from rural chimneys and a coyote or two to find the best place to sleep.

For a back rest, I prefer ponderosas, but a nice fir will do.

Firs are shadier, and because poderosas grow on open slopes, you're likely to get sun in your eyes when the flaming ball of heat cackles over the ridge imitating a Rhode Island rooster.

It wakes the best of us.

To avoid being lit up like a radon watch by the morning sun, look for a good canopy to block light and use it like the brim of a ball cap. Sometimes I hide in a patch of ocean spray or syringa.

My son doesn't have a preference yet.

He'll take to a stump as readily as a rock, or a road bank to break up his silhouette. Before long he's emitting turkey purrs as good as any professional talker of Osceola hens.

Those early morning romps through woody dreamlands have their drawbacks.

"Tom at two o'clock," I hissed at him last week.

"Puuurrrrrrr," he said back.

"Psst, it's almost in your lap!"

Earlier, a wild tom looking for a wild hen clattered loudly between the boy and me as we intermittently purred and yelped through solid REM before we sensed something was amiss. Then we jumped like twin Jack-in-the-boxes to our feet.

"Tom!" I howled.

"Dog gone!" My son chirped back, rubbing the sleep from his eyes.

We sent the gobbler looking for hens less large, wild eyed and armed as it raced out of sight through streams of sunshine and standing timber.

Don't worry about it, I yawned, slumping back to the ground. Sleeping in the woods has its travails, but it sure gets the eyelids fluttering on a gorgeous spring morning.

There will be more birds, I sleepily assured us both. So, let's hit a tree, or a stump, and the snooze button on our watches.

Outdoor sleeping is among the best of our family traditions.

Summer

Ball Busting Pend Oreille Bronzebacks

SANDPOINT — We're on the water, but barely. We are over the water, hovering, but not even that.

The engine is hollering.

The flesh of our faces is contorted. We are looking ahead into a wind wrought by our progress.

We are flat-ass flying.

As the seventeen-foot skiff, the three of us occupy, skims the glass surface of Lake Pend Oreille's north end the fiberglass hull skips while the boat's tail, and its stern and transom, bump the aqua velva blue just enough to keep the big engine shooting spray behind us like a fat-cheeked kid at a soda fountain.

"This thing does pretty good," the guy at the console, my unpaid and unrequited guide for the day shouts into the wind. I can almost see the bubble that carries his voice swish away behind him and out over the motor and the lake like a Chinese poem scribbled in a hurricane.

We are heading to Bottle Bay Resort because the gas gauge says empty and we know we need more fuel than what's in reserve to fish the many places that bass frequent on this massive, water-filled hole in the ground that sports a hundred miles of shoreline and dives to a thousand feet in places.

We started early and cast into fishy spots that included the cribbing of people's docks, a paddy-covered bay, a sand bar where a stream pushed icy mountain flows into the lake and we hoisted a few smallmouths that chased, grabbed and got hooked on barbell streamers with tails made of bunny fur.

By the time the gas light blinked, many lakeside residents hadn't had their first cup of coffee or even sniffered the lake air. They had not heard the spiraling laugh of the osprey or watched bumblebees dance on the rusty lilies at their front steps dappled with morning sun.

We however had dropped the boat into the lake before daybreak. Darkness was tested by a blinking neon sign on the highway near the boat launch.

"Showers and Laudromat," the sign said in a hundred small flashing bulbs before the first streak of morning light, like a refrigerator door cracked open, cut a slit over the Cabinet Range.

We could have burned a lot of fuel in the last three hours but our method of fishing didn't require it.

Our dearth of fuel began at the launch and was a result of one single inadequacy in a pile of things that were more than adequate.

Casting over sand bars, throwing streamers into the maw

of creeks, drifting, idling the electric motor into weedy bays, slamming fur and feathers into pond water shallows and watching bass wheel out of the murk, bronze backed, mouths agape, to bend fly rods, or leave only a bulge and a boil.

Those were adequate.

We had boxes of streamers in many colors and weights, with bulging eyeballs and hooks hidden in scads of fur and feathers, enough for a casting call of Voodoo Children.

And we had fly rods of different weights and lengths, with fly line weight forward and sinking, fat and skinny, bulging like a herniated duodenum or drawn out like the guts of indigenous bow strings.

All of it we had in quantities that exceeded adequate.

We just forgot to top off the gasoline tanks, that's all.

We had used fuel wisely to the point when the gas gauge began vying for attention. It was around the same time there arose a desire to scoot down the river west of town to some hot bassy spots.

Oh, to fall by virtue.

Because of this small inadequacy, Calvin, our unpaid guide, grins like he just guttered a ball and left one pin standing.

Calvin is at the wheel. He is not a guide although he is a former sporting goods store owner, who recently combined his venture with another, and the new enterprise allows him to fish more than before.

That's the word.

He now operates a fly fishing shop for Big R – the farm and ranch supply store – but with a twist. He gets to spend time showing people around, which helps to market the new venture.

That is why, in part, we are free wheeling across the big lake, almost hovering on the water, skipping, spitting a nominal amount of spray from under the hull as fly rods and fly gear lay piled on the boat's forward casting platform.

As we hydroplane over the lake's sheet metal surface a fuzzy, bunny-tail streamer with a barbell eye that lies on the deck is caught by the wind and skips overboard. Calvin, or Sam, the marketing guy at Big R who has joined us in this bass-getting junket, stab a hand in an attempt to catch the departing lure as the boat keeps rocketing toward the gas pumps at Bottle Bay.

Next, a big chicken feather streamer with a bullet head that was nestled under the rail of a gunwale lifts into the wind and tea kettles into the lake behind us.

Soon, another takes flight. This one is an articulated version with a peanut eye.

The unimpeded launching of gumbo streamers happens often enough for a passenger to wonder why we don't stop and stow the lures, but we don't. We keep going, flying rocketlike with contorted faces toward the gas pumps at Bottle Bay.

The lures, some of them stuck into the outdoor carpet that lines the boat, are loosed by the muscly wind. The white, black and green, fuzzy, furry or feathery streamers one at a time lift from the boat into the air and sail over the water, past outstretched hands like hard candy at a Fourth of July parade.

Calvin grins.

Sam smiles as if to shrug,

There is more where they came from, these curators of fly shops seem to say.

Sam brought many of the streamers from corporate headquarters in Great Falls, Montana, where they were invented and tied during long nights in the spring when the Missouri River was high. They are meant to catch brown trout on the Mo and their names — Flying Fudgsicle, Green Gobslobber, Naked Hula Dancer, all works in progress — pricked Sam's fly-fishing curiosity.

Interest piqued.

He asked himself the inevitable question:

"Will these whatchamajigs catch bass in Idaho?"

Earlier today, in the dark, after we launched, he handed them around and as the morning progressed we threw them at banks, lily pads and rip rap.

Bass, not huge, but plucky nonetheless, grabbed them and like small dogs at a barbecue, refused to heel.

It took a little prodding from the fly rods made especially for spiny rays to bring the fish to hand and let them go again.

Throwing streamers at bass was less novel than Calvin's and Sam's coming together.

Both men were anglers with different retail backgrounds.

Calvin ran a local sporting goods and fly shop while Sam had ties to a Montana-based farm and ranch supply chain.

Farm and ranch stores seem to engender a certain tropism that almost always drips pragmatism. Their fishing is worms, cane poles and a prairie tank, or at least a duct-taped spin rod plunking plastic worms as the nighttime chuckle of a poorwill, like a C note, vibrates through the thorny brush.

Sam's Big R isn't like that.

The shop in Ponderay, for instance, across the highway from Sandpoint, is a sort of novelty Big R made for a hunting and fishing crowd that also owns livestock and grows fruit trees, for instance. The store's sporting goods section abuts the hand-tool aisle, and mounted heads of burly elk silently watch customers rassling their feet into fresh out-of-the-box muck boots.

The fly shop here rivals those in Western towns known for their microbrews and blue ribbon trout rivers.

Both men seem to understand the future. It calls for catering to a more diverse crowd than only fly fishers or hay farmers. At this Big R, their needs are combined.

When we slide into Bottle Bay under the gaze of waterfront mansions, a shirtless man in shorts and flip-flops walks down the dock, yawning, to tell us the place has no fuel.

"Won't have any until the truck comes in a few hours," he says.

We shall not be dismayed.

The fuel gauge on the console is buzzing now like a gull with a craw full of hotdogs and Calvin, whose grin has not abated, turns the bow northwest and guns the engine, this time towards town.

We make it there and fuel up.

No big deal.

Then we fish the city canal, better known as Sand Creek,

which is dock and boat-laden. It passes under streets and gangways. The electric motor's battery is almost gone, and the big hundred and fifteen horsepower engine is asking for oil.

It has been one of those trips.

We slip quietly through shadows of the highway and railroad bridges as Calvin and Sam cast at pylons that carry the burden of commerce to this North Idaho town. When we reach a dock a half block from Main Street, they reel in.

Stepping onto the dock, we shake off the morning and head to MickDuff's Brewing Company for a soup, sandwich and maybe a beer.

There's more fishing to come.

For now, however, it has been decided that streamer chucking at North Idaho bronzebacks is best done on a full stomach and with a full tank of gas.

Big Bad Wolfe

ST. JOE CITY — He's wearing the white T-shirt and baggy logging jeans he always wears with his suspenders and Romeo slippers.

The sun is like a paper cut, stinging the asphalt alongside his single-wide trailer.

I park my pickup truck in a gravel parking space. His seven-year-old lab who I remember as a pup doesn't bother barking but looks at me laconically from a shady spot on the porch.

Rodney Wolfe wears a baseball cap he got from his kids or grandkids with a fishing logo that reads Old Anglers Don't Die They Just Lose Their Action, or something. He's got a pantry full of caps with similarly rancorous phrases all of them referring to fishers who have hit their prime.

"Just the man I've been looking for," he shouts from the kitchen when he sees me walk alongside his house that is isolated on a ridge with a view of the St. Joe River as it winds lazily through a valley near St. Joe City.

I called twice as I approached but he didn't hear.

"Lost my damned hearing aid," he says.

We walk to his small outside shop with its doors propped open.

"Move this battery for me, Stud," he commands. "Set it right there."

Rodney Wolfe is working on his boats again.

"Can you get that Jon boat down from the rafters?"

I climb a ladder.

"Help me load this pontoon here."

He flipped one in the river recently but it won't stop him from floating again.

Boats are a lot of what I've helped Rodney Wolfe with over the years at his home on the hill, and as a reward, he's always given me a liberal dose of fly dubbing and a raft of jocose raillery.

"How's your love life, Stud?"

He waits for an answer in an effort to reload the shotshell of his wit before bantering on.

"I had three wives, but only two were any good."

"How many kids you got?"

"Boy you beat me. You hit a homerun at every bat, didn't ya?"

"How's the fly tying coming?"

I spent one winter at his fly-tying vise learning a handful of patterns that caught fish, but I eventually drifted back to one I used most often and which tied easier than the rest, never graduating from the blue dun that he calls a Big Bad Wolfe. He uses it in slow water when the sun drives most anglers into the shade while he catches what he calls beautiful fish.

"I always caught my biggest fish in the heat of the day," he will tell.

He calls the Big Bad Wolfe his trout weapon. It was the first fly he invented long before he enlisted in the Big One and was sent to the jungles of the South Pacific.

"Before WWII we had very poor tying materials compared to now," he once wrote in a newspaper column called Fishing, Hunting, Lying that appeared for years in the St. Maries Gazette Record, a local tattler.

"The neighbor's rooster, JCPenney buttonhole thread and salvaged sweater yarn made up our supplies.

"Tyers with money could purchase hooks and better quality materials from Herter's. We had our own Rhode Island Red and cross roosters with ginger grizzly hackle."

At that time, in the late 1930s, there were giant mid-morning and early evening hatches of the Hexagenia mayfly, he will tell.

"After driving through the hatches, windshields would look as if they had fruit salad on them and the river would come alive with rising fish."

After the war, he started selling flies, and the Big Bad Wolfe was his best seller.

He sold his hand-tied patterns for thirty-five cents apiece, or $3.50 per dozen, at a gas station in St. Maries, the hangout of most of the area's fly fishermen.

Good flies were difficult to come by then, and although his

early models weren't pretty — rather crude, he says — they did catch the heck out of the huge population of trout in the St. Joe and St. Maries rivers.

He sold his patterns from roadside stands in the St. Joe National Forest until the federal government decided he needed a license. The regulation shut down his business in the forest, but it didn't stop him from informing anglers of the deadliness of his homemade flies.

"Once I was fishing in the nice hole just before Flemming Creek and caught a fine trout on nearly every cast," he wrote in one of his newspaper columns. "I broke the barb off my hook and those trout were so greedy for my Big Bad Wolfe fly that I had to hide behind a drooping cottonwood to change patterns."

His calling card hung in businesses from Avery to St. Maries and sometimes under the windshield wiper blades of cars parked along the river.

"St. Joe Dry Flys," the card read. "Barbless Hooks. C. Rodney Wolfe. Greatest Fisherman. Best Hunter. Biggest Liar in the St. Joe Valley."

Clients bit.

He sold gobs of his flies and kept making them until he surpassed 80 years old.

He still writes newspaper columns in long hand and sends them to the news desk to be typeset, which invariably prompts an intercom call asking the editor to visit the transcriber down the hall who is harried.

"Can you help me decipher this chicken scratch?"

He blames the squiggle on bad eyes and a hand unsteady at the pen, but still deft enough to tie a Big Bad Wolfe.

"It's hard to write when you're seeing double," he said.

Wolfe, who grew up in town when paddle wheelers tied up to the docks in St. Maries fished the panhandle's St. Joe before it was given the moniker "Shadowy St. Joe," and long before a man named Duane Hagadone penned "North Idaho" in his newspapers. Both terms are as common now as Keystone cans along any highway here.

Anyone who has waded the St. Joe River to cast caddis fly imitations into runouts in an effort to catch the river's ample cutthroat trout has heard of Wolfe.

Anglers who cast bead-head nymphs, streamers, or some other sinking variation of fake trout food, may have heard from him as well.

Wolfe is a dry fly purist who has worked fly patterns on the more than a hundred miles of fishable trout waters of the St. Joe since he was old enough to get his feet wet.

For Wolfe, fishing started as a necessity. He and his siblings caught trout to feed the family in the latter years of the Great Depression and he learned to tie flies from a riverboat girl who was fifteen years his senior. He had a crush on her and coaxed her with the flies he made.

"But Maggie's love wasn't for sale," he says, seventy years later.

Fly fishing grew into a passion.

In 1971, when he worked as a boiler attendant at a local sawmill Wolfe wrote a treatise on cutthroat trout.

It wasn't well received.

The longtime fisherman and fly tier was asked to present to a university fisheries class the twenty-page paper in which he called for a catch-and-release trout fishery on the upper St. Joe River. In the document, he criticized the state fishery department for stocking rainbow trout in waters where the fish weren't indigenous. According to the thesis, the stocking program would ruin the river's pure strain of west slope cutthroat trout. Rainbows and cutts hybridized, he wrote, relegating the pure, genetic west slopes to small populations of undersize fish in tiny tributaries that rainbows didn't inhabit.

The lecture, he said, was a lesson in humility.

"I was almost laughed out of the classroom," he said.

The professor ridiculed his lack of erudition and a college degree, and derided Wolfe for possessing no formal science training.

"I never came so close to hitting a man with glasses," said Wolfe.

But, like a hook before the barb is bent down, the management Wolfe asked for, eventually stuck.

Almost thirty years later much of what he wrote became policy on the St. Joe River.

Within the last decade, citing cost and limited survival rates, Idaho quit stocking rainbows in the St. Joe. The state of wild, west slope cutthroat trout in waterways where they once were as common as caddis flies has become a regional priority as well. Several organizations have called for stringent cutthroat trout regulations to ensure the survival of the pure strain, native fish that lives mostly in the river's tributaries.

"You can't hardly find them anymore," Wolfe says.

On this day, he plans to fish for bass, he says, and wants to be on the water by noon.

The sun bristles.

"Bass don't bite when it's hot like this, so I won't have to clean any," he says.

I hear later that he broke the lower unit off his outboard motor when he rolled the boat and the trailer off a too-steep launch.

I call to ask about the mishap.

"Geezus!" I exclaim.

Without missing a tick, he quips.

"Jesus had nothing to do with it."

There are many solid, and some expert fly fishers on the St. Joe, but most of them hit the waters weekends, a time when Wolfe won't go near the river.

Too many tubers and hot rodders.

"There isn't enough room to put my boat in," he says.

The once lean and able angler who has waded the river in its entirety and most of its tributaries, often uses a jon boat now to fish the slower sections between Calder and Marble Creek.

Sometimes he'll sit in a lawn chair, knee deep in the river and cast.

"Can't take the cold water like I used to," he says.

He doesn't complain about limited access or mobility,

choosing instead to chase trout on less populous sections of his favorite stream.

Most anglers leave the river's lower portions alone. They don't know the intricacies of the water, every rock wall, bubble line, nick and spring for miles that Wolfe learned as a boy fishing by himself, hopping the Milwaukee Line that used to skirt a great length of the St. Joe and its cousin the North Fork.

Wolfe is getting a pacemaker and plans to be back fishing by August when his strength is back.

After meeting with him for coffee at a local café we mill in the parking lot before saying goodbye.

The sky is gray and Wolfe is dressed in his sack-like logger jeans, suspenders, the trademark red woolen cruiser jacket and a baseball cap with something close to an obscene logo reflecting his favorite pastime.

For years the local kids called him "Redneck Rod," for the crewcuts he sported and his willingness to dispense sage advice on any topic.

As he climbs into his pickup, he fills the silence with a favorite phrase.

"If you run into any trouble," he gruffs. "Don't let it stop you."

He slams the door, fires the engine and drives away.

Lindsey and His Lakers

PRIEST LAKE — Rich Lindsey keeps a wire cutter in a cup holder in the back of his boat.

It's a pocket-size cutter used to dislodge fouled hooks and to snip tangled leaders.

And it's used to kill fish.

The killing is done with swift dexterity and a mantra.

A mackinaw — the fish his clients hire him to help them catch — is held with one hand by its gill slits as clients admire its lines, size, V-tail and verticulation. The other hand, the one Lindsey uses to grasp the implement, makes one or two swift movements as the dull steel knot of the wire cutter thumps the fish between the eyes.

As one of the Panhandle's premier fishing guides, a guy who has been at it longer than anyone in this northern land of woods and mountains that plunge into the gem-like lakes of prehistoric glacial gouges, Lindsey has his own way of doing things.

"Welcome aboard," he lilts softly from underneath a walrus-style mustache as the fish with each thump extends its fins like oriental fans. The lake trout quiver and their eyes pop skyward. Clouds race over their sheeny skin as brain pans are irreparably jostled.

The fish are dropped into a box near the transom with a cutting board top and although Idaho Fish and Game allows anglers to keep six lake trout, Lindsey's boat limit is three apiece. The smaller limit gives clients enough of the succulent pink-fleshed fish to feed a family and ensures his home waters keep on giving.

"This lake has been generous to me," Lindsey says.

His generosity gives clients a taste of North Idaho's Valhalla while keeping the lake fertile from a piscatorial perspective.

As fishery management programs in many northern Idaho lakes preclude any mention of mackinaw or lake trout, unless it is to be rid of them, Priest Lake in the state's northern reaches — so far north that it keeps the riff raff out, as some residents like to proclaim — is a different ball game.

Anglers visit from afar for a chance at one of Lindsey's lakers, the big ones that will bend a rod as Lindsey shouts, "Reel, reel, reel!" He expounds these sentiments into the cool, seemingly motionless air as the sports stand splay-legged in the back of his boat like eager swains at the crossroads of exhilaration and anxiety.

The name of the game is simple: Hook and haul lake trout to the surface and then to the net. Big ones if you can, and that's what Lindsey and his clients do.

My own obsession with mackinaw began as a kid on a northern lake where I grew up.

I fished for bass mostly, and walleye during the full-moon nights of July and August. Muskie could be found in the spring and fall and northern pike were caught in the evening pulling plugs off the rock ledges where they hunted.

Lake trout were an anomaly that existed mostly in my dreams.

They hung deep, in water of seventy feet or more, out there in Big Bay, paddling their V-tails in the black, haunted depths often white-capped and swollen with mystery.

I caught one as a fourteen-year-old jigging for walleye like my Uncle Jim taught me. As my line dangled off a reef and the waves slapped the side of my Crestliner, blowing it off course, I hooked a split tail trout that fought like a walleye. I reeled the fish up and into the boat before admiring it and letting it go. I was unsure of the rules, or whether by keeping it I would deny the lake its future brood stock.

The fish I pulled from the depths was speckled with small scales. Its eyes were not glazed like shop-window glass — the sign of a walleye.

It came up slowly from the cold, deep water like a walleye does and it had similar spike teeth, but this fish offered an aura of its own

"Lake trout," I said out loud, almost whistling, as waves lapped the aluminum hull. I pulled the fish in for a better look.

This was catch-and-release fishing before it was cool and the beginning of an idea that said, unless you require the protein, throwing fish back allows for catching them again. Maybe more of them.

The entertainment was better than cable TV and the lessons couldn't be had in a school room.

We know this now.

Fishing was mostly diversion, but not keeping the catch garnered my mother's reproof. To deflect criticism I carried the occasional bass and panfish home on a stringer and sometimes a pike that was hooked too deep.

These alms kept me in fishing licenses and boat gas until I was old enough for a job.

Being on the water became respite and a necessity.

Lindsey's commitment is more robust.

He tells of a forty-pound mack he caught while fishing alone and the trial of shooting a picture with his cell phone camera before letting the beast free to spawn again, and hopefully be hooked by one of his clients on another occasion.

He has a picture for proof and as advertising, but the catch and release almost cost him the cell phone he used to take the picture.

"Those big ones are surly," he says. "When they start slapping their tails, you gotta drop 'em overboard."

Releasing the tail slappers, watching them fin lethargically into the dark adds solace to otherwise exciting days with clients. It ensures the big boys and girls will be around to spawn like a living, breathing trout factory building a more boisterous community.

It is what Lindsey wants to believe.

The fishery department's efforts, however, to rid state waters of the speckled, deep-water gargantuans by netting, tracking and eradicating them for the sake of other species they deem more worthy, native or lucrative, begins anew each winter.

About the time Lindsey starts filling his calendar with clients who want a piece of the mackinaw action, state-paid commercial trawlers are pulling nets through spawning pods of the species he and his clients deem most valuable.

The state catches and kills mackinaws while Lindsey's sports, the ones who view macks with awe, call him on his cell phone, leave email messages, book dates and lay down payments.

They will — some have dreamed it for years — drive a thousand miles to Idaho's northwesternmost corner to lock horns with a laker on the Gem State's last great mackinaw water.

They wait at the dock wearing floppy hats.

They smile.

They shake hands with their fishing guide and when the sun rises, wrapping the mooring with orange and pink cellophane, they rub sunscreen on their naked arms, necks and faces, calming nerves bundled with anticipation.

"Think we'll catch a big one?" they ask from under broad brims.

Lindsey smiles through his trademark stache and adjusts his baseball cap.

"Only one way to find out," he softly sings.

Junkies of the Joe

Dan at the Idaho Fly Fishing Company asks if I want a coffee.

My fishing partner offered to purchase flies, line and whatnot because I paid for gas and provided the wheels to drive the eighty miles to our favorite hole.

Once we approach middle age, discounts, like the coupons your aunt kept in a cookie jar and laid on the counter like solitaire, suddenly seem essential.

We stop at Dan's because it's halfway to where we're going and we like his ribbing and advice.

He overheard the payment plan.

"How about a twenty-ounce triple Americano," he winks from behind the counter, his cheeks red as Santa's from river sun and last night's Sangria with pals on the deck of the fly shop that overlooks the river and the mayflies hatching.

"I'll put a chunk of ice in it for you."

Mottern is an aficionado of many things. He knows the Latin names of bugs, trout and how to find the perfect elk hunting spot using Google Earth. He prepares sandwiches like DaVinci, scoops ice cream with the flair of a carnival barker, spools line on fly reels with his eyes closed as he hums Rachmaninov, and he grinds beans and brews Joe — the dark, steamy kind that keeps you awake as the yellow line of the road unspools like a downwind cast.

Coffee, he knows, is as much a part of this thing we call fly fishing as garters at a high school prom.

It's the universal tire iron required to change a flat on a one-lane trail overlooking a thousand feet of mist and river. It's the juice under the straw, the punch in Hawaiian and it sips away time as miles slip under the big lug tires of our pickup trucks.

The river today is sun-scattered and cold. If you miss the abrupt swing into a parking spot at Dan's shop you'll drive straight into its current.

Dan waits. His espresso machine burps.

"We have hand-tied flies, beautiful big stimmies, local literature and a brand new batch of fishing boots," he chortles. "And local art ... We got art. What's your pleasure?"

My arm feels suddenly twisted.

"Sure," I chirp. "I'll have that triple with a chip of ice, and I'll stop back later for the rest."

Driving through Coeur d'Alene one will find a robust array of coffee stops tastefully perched on virtually every street corner with newly-painted curbing.

Drive out of town and coffee stops are hit and miss.

Les Vawter at the Junction Conoco at Rose Lake has the

stuff that is pure caffeine, but his regular coffee is more aromatic. He keeps it in canisters, filled and freshly brewed. It goes well with the deep-fried egg and ham breakfast wraps that disappear sometime between first light and the morning mail.

When we drive over Lookout Pass to hit the Montana side of some Idaho rivers we take the twenty-ounce cups of Les' coffee to ensure we're vibrant with quality brew.

We have fished past DeBorgia, skipping dry flies on icy cold streams from snowcaps with Les' coffee still hot and invigorating as we traveled east.

Drive through The Maries and the gas station at the edge of town called Ed's has its own version. Bring the same cup back and a refill costs a quarter. Notch the cups to the visor with a bobby pin and the change from underneath the floor mat will tide you over each time you're there.

Shift and Grind, the local brew stand, should be on your GPS.

A tavern off the interstate at Enaville where the beer cans and nightcrawlers share the same cooler, also serves coffee in styrofoam cups.

"You fly fish?" a guy asked while warming a Rainier with a paw like a catcher's mitt. He used to elegantly cast emergers and the dainty paraduns of winter hatches, he confided. It's mostly spinners now.

"I use a snap-on swivel," he grinned. "I don't need to see to set the hook."

In Lewiston on the way to an autumn river, or driving

into the snow-dusted hills after chukar, ask for a tray and
have the baristas at Hot Shot Espresso fill each slot with
triple shots. The coffee is as remarkable as the surroundings
are resplendent.

Once, at Melrose on the Big Hole, we followed guys with
Wranglers and western hats into the tavern. In early spring
we wore rubber pants and stocking caps. We expected at least
one remark that compared us to DEVO, but the bartenders
simply asked if the brown trout were cooperating. One
guy whose face was a geological survey, and whose Sunday
polyester slacks and brush popper shirt complemented a pair
of pointed boots, had seen a hatch of callibaetis.

"They ain't many," the man said, sipping a Moscow Mule
from a copper cup. "But they's comin' up."

We ordered big coffees and returned to the river where we
tied on tiny mayfly imitations.

I have no preference when it comes to java except that it's
flavorful and there's plenty of it.

If I get a cup of re-prod swill, made from double poured
water over double-used grounds, I ain't comin' back.

It happens sometimes in out-of-the-way places where
employees keep the corn dogs in the hot case for a week and
the beef burritos will break your teeth. Some local haunts
have fallen off our radar for their lack of grace and ribald
culinary inclinations. The coffee reeks of roof melt brewed
through cedar shakes.

We will drive through another state to avoid those places.

As gas prices reach epicurean highs and every long drive

requires contingencies, coupons and the charity of others, a carafe of good Joe is as vital as new radials.

A stout set of tires in the hinterlands will keep the ditch away, and a traveler may go for hours on a refill of swell brew.

Night Fishing

Night fishing on a lake not far from Canada under a July moon will make your synapses crackle like a Mylar balloon.

Stand on a dock in the moon's melon-colored light with mosquitos caroling in your ears and throw a Hula Popper near the rocky shore you cannot see, but that you know exists. Hear the lure splash when it strikes the water and then wait. Give it a slow retrieve, just a couple of turns on the reel while twitching your rod tip. Let the lure float freely in the black shadows of birch and ash for several seconds before guiding it, again easily, just a few turns, into the strip of moonlit water where you let it float. Hold on. Be patient. Then, with a wrist twitch, give it a pop. The sound — the lure's namesake — comes from the rounded, embossed lips that resemble a toilet seat and which grab air like a jug band.

The sound attracts feeding bass, which find the intrusion of a bullfrog-like interloper in their territory an affront to their jailhouse demeanor.

They become homicidal.

Retrieve the aptly named Hula Popper easily once more, letting it crawl on the water's surface into the dark pale of nighttime hush.

Somewhere between the farthest and nearest point, with a few jerks from the rod tip that make the lure mimic the deep bassoon-like plunk of a frog in the throes of a mating cycle, a smallmouth bass will shoot from the black water and strike the lure with such ferocity it will send your lungs into your throat.

The bronzy fish will swirl unseen from a black hole slamming the plug with a gulp and a resounding splash that, in a night otherwise calm as an Italian chapel, is akin to a volcano blast in your heart. The concussion rockets up your spine but is denied exit through the top of your skull.

The metallic salt of adrenaline is dizzying and immediately addictive. Your hair sizzles and your eyes tip back like a faith healing as you grip the rod and reel to your chest with both hands.

The bass that ate the Hula Popper shakes and splashes. It lunges deep then shoots up and out of the water making the dark world around you come full stop like the end of a pirouette.

Your knees are locked and the soles of sockless sneakers test their grip on the lumber of an old dock made of cedar poles and planks.

Mosquitoes probe your ankles. The aroma of damp cedar fills your nostrils along with the warm murk of algae and dead mayflies. The water was still as a spotted fawn until the bass shattered the surface. The rings catch moonlight.

The only thing out here, many miles from the nearest mini-mart, that remotely gives a nod to humanity are two, red, blinking lights on a forested rise miles away across the lake.

The lights, nebulous and distant, provide a sense of isolation as you stand on the wood planking under a limpid moon like the Rousseau painting of two clowns wearing dunce caps.

It's whimsical and solitary, this night fishing, until the pulse of a bass driving wildly through your lure introduces you to catharsis and cold blood.

Heading to the safety of deep water the bass endeavors to pull the rod from your hands as it throbs along the lake's rocky shoals.

Steadily, you conduct this orchestra with your fishing rod baton, recalling how once you witnessed a smallmouth launch like a trident missile, red-eyed and wild after striking an Arbogast original jitterbug in broad daylight. It cut blue air, fanning a rainbow-colored spray, a treble hook lodged deeply into its fleshy jaw. You imagine now the inverse happening under a drip from the moon, the bass black-sided with amethyst eyes, the spray like coal dust, the air tarnished copper.

The brazen howl of mosquitoes and the maniacal fraying of your senses help you decipher what's next.

As the fish fights the hook near the dock, you consider calling for assistance, just a hand to maneuver a flashlight but you are alone. Other guests are inside the cabin up a path through the trees. The cabin's window is a postage stamp of incandescent light.

Calling out would break the spell and invite disaster. At the very least it would deflate the sensuality of this enterprise.

Only you have experienced the intensity of the last few minutes. A flashlight gingerly fished from your back pocket is snapped on. The rod butt is pinched under an elbow. The beam cuts into the lake as the fish fins by. You reef the smallmouth into the shaft of light and it floats quietly in the pollen-speckled water. Its gills pulse.

There it is.

That is the beast that caused you such delight.

Not much of a beast really, not now. You estimate it weighs two and a half pounds, maybe three. You kneel on the dock's cedar planks — they are springy — and reach down as the smallmouth bolts away splashing you, but you have it now like a panting dog on a short leash. Mosquitoes are in your ear, they dance on bare arms as you lay on the dock with a hand thrust toward the fish. Flashlight in your mouth, you pull the bass out face first and gripping its lower lip you unhook and let the smallmouth go.

Illuminated, it hangs for a moment in the placid current near the dock's peeled cribbing as if unsure of its freedom. Then it brusquely flips its tail and disappears into a darkness your light cannot fathom.

The experience has exhilarated both angler and fish, you surmise, as you pick your way along the stony path through grass and bat traffic to the lodge lighted by a kerosene lamp and a bare bulb over a table by the window.

Night fishing for walleye on big lakes that turn monstrous under the uneven light of the Milky Way raises another kind of awareness.

When windchimes jingle from the porches of island cottages after Army- surplus generators have shut off and window lights have dimmed, the eery peal sends the electricity of anticipation pulsing through your limbs.

The sun lights another continent beyond the hump of the earth's lenticular curve and elsewhere a moon might be hanging in a pine. Mosquitoes don't venture over the water unless they are shanghaied under a boat seat or bow cover, so their terrible whining doesn't reach your ears. The only sound, before the wind strikes this hush-hush-like secrecy, is from a hook or sinker dropped on the aluminum hull, a reel cranking, a mushroom anchor accidentally kicked, or an angler's cigarette cough in the dark.

When the wind chimes on nearby islands jingle it lets fishers know what's next.

Soon, from the ink night a half mile away gulls are blown off their perch on a pile of rocks. You hear them complain before the rushing vortex of wind catches trees on the nearby islands. Waves pushed by the wind suddenly splash on shorelines and tumble into the quiet alcove where you drift over a thirty-foot reef like a weather balloon. The abrupt white-capped waves glow in the night like shark teeth. They noisily bump the boat's hull. The interruption is swift and frightening even though you expected it.

The northerly at twenty-two hundred Zulu time is a common July phenomenon and lets you know when to turn on the running lights, reel in, stow the gear, and crank the engine before awkwardly angling home on a following sea.

Night fishing on rivers is a Tasmanian devil. It is sinister and a little dangerous for waders who step one foot at a time off the bank into the invisible current. If the river is placid and lovely at dusk, it has the potential to be quarrelsome and toothy by starlight before it turns gorgeous again as your body conforms to its after-dark secrets.

Once, at a tavern that has since burned down, along a local river that is slowly being polluted by well-meaning summer visitors — the bane of beautiful things — I sat with a man who listened to complaints from a group of out-of-state anglers who bemoaned the river's small fish. Its blue-ribbon status demanded a larger quarry, the men lamented, and the river's native cutthroat trout at the height of summer were not overly accommodating.

The man next to me emptied the bottle of beer he had nursed.

"Maybe they ought to fish at night," he said, leaving his stool.

I followed him to the gravel parking lot. It was dusk and fat bugs ping-ponged around the nearest street light.

"Night fishing?" I asked, having read that bigger fish, like whitetail bucks, prefer to feed when no one's harassing them.

"The biggest ones travel at night," he said before driving

his two-toned and sun-blistered pickup truck across the pot-holed parking lot to the highway through a slick of summer twilight.

Not much later, my friend Tim and I employed the tactic strategically and without fanfare.

We told no one except our boss at the newspaper who grinned and pushed a hand through his hair.

We drove upstream for almost an hour at dusk with our flyrods loaded and ready for action held tight by the wiper blades, and when we got to the stretch of river we planned to fish we could barely see the road for the insect genocide — a curtain of exploded thoraxes — on our windshield.

And because it was dark.

It dawned on us, but not very brightly, that the rutted path down the steep embankment to the river would be unlit, just like the water.

The headlamps we wore worked marvelously if we wanted a look at our hands or shoes, otherwise, they bored into the pool of darkness like it was chocolate pudding.

We shut them off, then fell down the hill from the road to the river, checked our rod tips to make sure they were attached and slipped into the black, roaring water like tritons. We were ready for whatever action the river could muster, barring death or bodily injury.

We were prepared to catch fish, which seemed fantastically heroic and clandestine and when car headlamps passed on the road we sniggered.

"Behold! Not a soul fathoms we're here."

Even our language changed.

"Where art thou, oh Theosophus?" And, "Did you grab the beer?"

It didn't matter. We lost track of each other.

Like pulpiteers of a new religion, we cast lusciously into the black noise of rushing water for hours, set adrift in the artful business of hooking night fish.

When we returned to the car our eyes were dish plates and our mouths were the obtuse hollows of lobed gauges.

"Wow," is all our vocal cords could muster as moonlight splashed against the thin thread of the highway.

The Last Of The Free Merc-Eteers

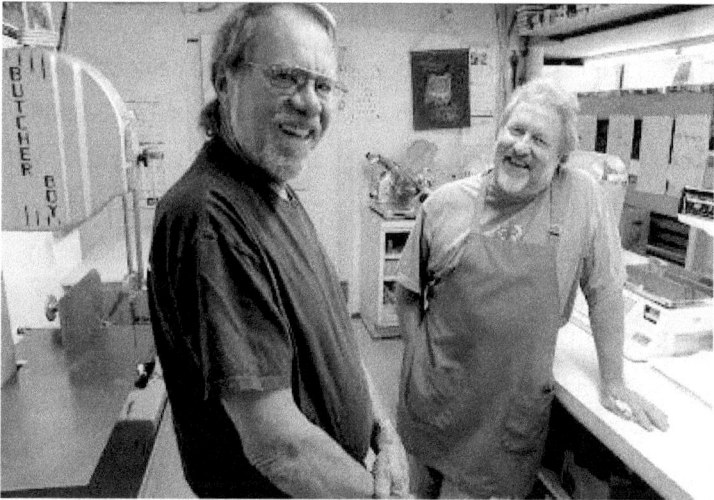

FERNWOOD — Don and Jay are bagging it, and we're not talking about groceries.

The two men have operated the Fernwood Mercantile, known as The Merc, south of St. Maries since moon boots were the latest rage.

They began working in the grocery store slash hardware and haberdashery in the 1970s when logging trucks carried the fine dust from the woods on their wheels and the whole highway corridor was powdery all summer with the perfume of bark and chips and pitch.

The store sold groceries and cut and wrapped your deer and elk meat in the fall, or whenever you brought one by. It sold booze and bronze pipe fittings, saw parts, suspenders and dungarees.

If you needed a stove pipe, Jay would grab a long-handled stick with a hook that could reach the pipe pieces that hung on the back wall above the Ajax. He lowered sections of stovepipe gingerly, blew the dust off and gave you a deal because many of the pieces had been hanging up there since Nixon was in office.

When I met this duo twenty years ago they were out back with a spud gun shooting potatoes across neighbors' ornamental trees, two city streets and into a cow pasture by the elementary school.

Ka-thunk went the guns after the men used a Bic lighter to ignite the hair spray that fueled the venture.

They were grown men but laughed like boys every time a big russet smacked a cow pie a hundred yards out.

The store, which also sells fuel, tube socks and a modest assortment of microbrew has survived in this community since 1913.

Don's grandfather bought it in the early 1950s, making Don third generation.

Since he and Jay took over, the venture has been great guns.

Which is expected — this being the lower reaches of Benewah County where guns, great, or small enough to carry in your pocket, are common as buttons on a pet vest.

"It drives the tourists crazy," says Don.

Burly men with beards and fowling pieces carried over shoulders as they consider pork chops in the meat department, or the big sidearm hanging from the holster of a smiling woman who is pressing the melons looking for the sweetest ones, gives tourists the jitters.

"They always ask, is that an undercover cop?"

He laughs.

"I tell them, you ain't in Warsh-ington no more."

The odd and audacious, Benewah-style, are so commonplace in this store, the town's centerpiece, that the owners of The Merc no longer recognize peculiarities.

One Sunday afternoon a while back, says Don, the mercantile was lit up with bikers, tweakers, loggers, churchgoers and a few Crypts from Yakima. When Jay walked in he stopped, gazed around, then sidled up to Don and quietly asked, "Does this place look like the bar scene in Star Wars?"

Don peered at the customers.

"I hadn't noticed it," he said. "Jay was right on the money."

After decades of working seven days per week and holidays, the two men are bagging it. They sold the business to a nice Tacoma couple.

"We've been standing on concrete for thirty-five years," Don says.

No more wearing the red or blue denim aprons and leaning

behind the meat counter sharing jokes. No more taking hits of moonshine from a canning jar that a covert distiller down the road dropped by for a tasting.

There will be no pranks or potato guns, and the hand-lettered signs purveying the kind of fly-over humor underappreciated on the outer coasts will come down from prominent perches above the vegetable aisle.

Foreseeing twenty-four hours each day the unblemished boxes of their respective calendars, the inevitable question arises.

What will they do with their free time?

Don and Jay pause. Grins creep garishly like zucchini vines over the men's unshaven faces.

They have known the answer all along.

"Whatever our wives let us," one of them ventures.

This makes them laugh aloud as if the remark itself welcomes mischief.

The playfulness is infectious. Nearby customers, acquainted with the men's good nature, smile too.

Years, Actually

HARRISON — My oldest daughter was blonde and in diapers when I last fished here. It was summer, the lake was lower, and the shoreline was silted and knuckled in driftwood. Rotting mayfly carcasses piled in the shade under the cottonwoods where water had receded and ducks with second broods idled in the marshy backwater gabbling and diving for snails.

It had been a long time since the last time I fished here. Years, actually. My oldest daughter now wears her hair purple or school-mascot red. She is vying for a driver's license and pines about the small incongruities that threaten to blot her high school "career."

Back then, on that August day, two years old, she was lathered in sunscreen, her cheeks bulged, no shirt to her shorts, and wearing saltwater sandals she touched with an extended finger the bright sunfish we pulled from the water. She giggled and ran back and forth to slide a stubby index finger along the sides of each fish until we caught the small pike. Its gnarled jaw and spike teeth made her scream and run for her mother's arms, tears glimmering on her red cheeks.

Today, I dropped her off at the park. School was out and she needed to measure the freedom she pined for and had read about all winter in the novels she lugged in her backpack. The freedom she envisioned while watching young people on television bore no resemblance to anyone's future.

She had her cell phone and iPod, small scepters of conformity with daily affirmations to the status quo.

Her fly rod leaned in the woodshed back home where I stashed it after a casting lesson a year ago.

Mom will pick me up, she said, before leaving with two boys her age who looked like night shift busboys at a downtown dive.

I drove the two youngest siblings, five and six years old, north out of town on the highway.

They were glum.

Why can't we go to the park? They asked. I want to go to the park.

You don't want to fish?

No, they chimed.

For them, being of the same mind was as rare as rain on a sunny day.

A few miles later we stopped along a side road to watch an osprey through binoculars.

Osprey, I said. Or, fishhawk.

Their spirits picked up.

A kingbird bobbed its tail and swooped from a power line, kingfishers darted, chattering. The sun charted the asphalt and the air smelled of water.

The planking on the steel bridge spanning the river pounded under our tires as we rolled over to the road at the edge of the lake raising fine, floury dust.

In a wide spot where the shoulder met the lake's pebbled shoreline, not far from where my oldest daughter, in diapers, had feared the pike, I threaded hooks with worms as the kids squinted listlessly into the afternoon sun.

Who will catch the first fish? I asked.

Me, they said.

Who will catch the biggest fish?

I will.

No, I will.

No you won't.

Just watch.

You don't know how.

Better than you, huh, dad?

Biggest fish gets a quarter, I said. The bobbers plopped near a weed bed and there was much talk of the largest fish and how many at once, and of another time at a different lake where we hooked fish after fish after fish. The kids scrounged the shoreline for sticks to use as faux fishing poles, they built a pretend fire ring in the road and filled it with leaves and roasted pretend marshmallows and as their bobbers dipped and I called them to reel, they grew older and stern and gave each other advice.

They dragged fish through weeds, broke some off, jibbered, jabbered, and held high the ones they landed. They asked to eat the perch and bluegills and we let each of the bright sunfish and the slim yellow perch back after much negotiation, petting and holding and getting thumbs pricked on dorsal spines.

Is that a poky fish, dad? They asked when more pint-size trophies were landed and the sun edged slowly to the tree line as shadows crossed the road. The water, which had sloshed with waves earlier, laid down flat as sheet metal.

We hooked a fish that ran out into the deep water and my son lowered the pole's tip. I carefully raised the rod's end, loosened the drag and he got the fish near the weeds before it dove and ran, unspooling with vigor the four-pound test line.

Nearer to shore the line bumped back and the big fish was gone. Reeling in, a small perch, its eyes bugged, its body tooth marked and ragged-finned, looked like it had emerged from a nightmare at the end of the hook.

Pike must have grabbed him, I said.

The kids agreed and played out the scene in the road as I reeled in the lines and packed up.

Look how big your eyes are.

You're scared.

I'm the pike, not you.

Do we have to go? They asked.

It's getting late, I replied.

Aw.

Which one of us caught the biggest fish?

Both of you.

I think she did, the boy said.

You, said the girl.

You both earned a quarter, I said.

Let's get ice cream, they shouted.

Our tires raised dust and drummed the wooden planks of the steel bridge.

We headed back, jibbering, jabbering, loaded with fish tales and a promise to return soon to this lake, and more often.

Maybe next week.